Acc **023357**
Class. 823.8
EL1

Preface Books

A series of scholarly and critical studies of major writers, intended for those needing modern and authoritative guidance through the characteristic difficulties of their work to reach an intelligent understanding and enjoyment of it.

General Editor: MAURICE HUSSEY

A Preface to Wordsworth	JOHN PURKIS
A Preface to Donne	JAMES WINNY
A Preface to Jane Austen	CHRISTOPHER GILLIE
A Preface to Yeats	EDWARD MALINS
A Preface to Pope	I.R.F. GORDON
A Preface to Hardy	MERRYN WILLIAMS
A Preface to James Joyce	SYDNEY BOLT
A Preface to Hopkins	GRAHAM STOREY
A Preface to Conrad	CEDRIC WATTS
A Preface to Lawrence	GĀMINI SALGĀDO
A Preface to George Eliot	JOHN PURKIS
A Preface to Auden	ALLAN RODWAY
A Preface to Dickens	ALLAN GRANT
A Preface to Shelley	PATRICIA HODGART
A Preface to Keats	CEDRIC WATTS

A Preface to George Eliot

John Purkis

Longman, London and New York

LONGMAN GROUP LIMITED
*Longman House
Burnt Mill, Harlow, Essex CM20 2JE, England
and associated companies throughout the world*

© Longman Group Limited 1985

All rights reserved. No part of this publication may be reproduced, stored in a retrieval system, or transmitted in any form or by any means, electronic, mechanical, photocopying, recording or otherwise, without the prior written permission of the Publishers.

First published 1985

British Library Cataloguing in Publication Data

Purkis, John
   A preface to George Eliot.—(Preface books)
   1. Eliot, George—Criticism and interpretation
   I. Title   II. Series
   823'.8   PR4688

ISBN 0-582-35277-0
ISBN 0-582-35278-9 Pbk

Set in 10/11pt Baskerville, Linotron 202

Produced by Longman Group (FE) Ltd
Printed in Hong Kong

JOHN PURKIS is the author of *A Preface to Wordsworth* in the same series. He is Staff Tutor in the East Anglian Region of the Open University. His most recent publication is *The World of the English Romantic Poets* (1982).

Contents

LIST OF ILLUSTRATIONS	vii
FOREWORD	viii
INTRODUCTION	ix
LIST OF ABBREVIATIONS AND STANDARD REFERENCES	x

PART ONE: THE NOVELIST IN HER SETTING	1
Chronological table	4
1 *A provincial life*	11
Robert Evans and his England	11
Childhood and schooltime	19
Intellectual awakening	22
2 *The religious crisis of the nineteenth century*	27
Doubts and difficulties	27
Church and chapels	28
Phrenology	34
The right books at the right time	39
The Religion of Humanity	45
3 *Choosing*	49
Alone in Geneva	49
John Chapman and the *Westminster Review*	51
Herbert Spencer and the study of society	53
Love and Mr Lewes	55
4 *Towards fiction*	59
Realism	59
Wordsworth and the power of memory	65
Becoming George Eliot	67
5 *Later years*	70
Showing that old acquaintances are capable of surprising us	70
Music and poetry	73
Finale	76
The idea of a future life	78

PART TWO: CRITICAL SURVEY	81
6 '*The Natural History of German Life*'	83
Prose extract: The historical conditions of society . . .	85

Prose extract: Shepperton Church — 88

7 *The transformation of reality: 'Amos Barton' to Adam Bede* — 92
Prose extract: . . . a sort of backstairs influence . . . — 102

8 *Contrasting heroines: Maggie and Romola* — 105
Prose extract: A variation of Protestantism — 116

9 Felix Holt *and* Middlemarch *as political novels* — 121
Prose extract: Felix in action — 128
Prose extract: A meditation upon the life of Saint Theresa — 130

10 *Constructing* Middlemarch — 133
Prose extract: The two sisters — 139

11 *Character in* Middlemarch — 143
Prose extract: The hospital vote — 147

12 *The achievement of* Middlemarch — 150

13 *The modernity of* Daniel Deronda — 152

PART THREE: REFERENCE SECTION — 157

A note on the word 'Original' — 159
Gazetteer — 161
Brief biographies — 173
Further reading — 179

APPENDIX — 184

Some letters from Robert and Isaac Evans — 184

ACKNOWLEDGEMENTS — 192

INDEXES — 193

List of Illustrations

Coventry by Turner	cover
George Eliot by Sir Frederic William Burton, 1865	frontispiece
Family tree of the Evans family	2
Robert Evans by Carlisle, 1842	12
Dinah Morris Preaching on the Green by Edward Henry Corbould	32
Phrenological head	35
Christ by Bertel Thorvaldsen, 1821	40
George Eliot by Francois D'Albert—Durade 1850	50
G. H. Lewes from a watercolour by Anne Gliddon c. 1840	56
Christ in the house of his parents by John Everett Millais, 1850	61
A Woman Scraping Parsnips by Nicholas Maes, 1655	63
The Priory, North Bank, St John's Wood	71
The Hireling Shepherd by William Holman Hunt, 1851	84
Chilvers Coton Church, engraving from the Illustrated London News, 1881	89
Hetty Sorrel, steel-engraving after Jozef Israels	99
Sacred and Profane Love by Titian	100
The Burning of the Vanities by Mrs Jane Benham Hay	110
The Visible Madonna by Frederic Leighton	112
Interior of St Michael's Church, Coventry by David Gee, 1862. A scene from provincial life	120
Nottingham Castle set on fire in the Reform Riots of 1832	127
Mr Brooke's miscellaneous dinner-party	136
Some relationships in *Middlemarch*	137
Manuscript page from *Middlemarch*; opening of Chapter 1	138
George Eliot's England	160
View from the bridge at Misterton Soss photographed by Gwil Owen	163
George Eliot's Coventry	166–169
Plan of a cottage by Robert Evans	191

vii

Foreword

George Eliot's intense dedication to the craft of fiction and the popularity and extreme versatility of the genre in the Victorian period made her into a writer of immense depth. She became in turn a literary countrywoman, a valued entertainer, a remarkable scholar and, finally, a seer and sage. To meet all these personae John Purkis has restated a number of the traditional estimates of her artistic procedures and stature but livened everything with his own sudden insights in the manner of the best volumes in this series.

Eliot's desire to work from man's social roots and duties left her at times a little apologetic towards some of her fictional rustics and their dimly understood superstitions. Yet these were still the substance of the organic culture of her day. Mr Purkis has studied the early rural novels especially for their human wisdom and as stations on the way to 'Middlemarch' or Coventry whose approach is shown in the painting by Turner that so appropriately enfolds the book. In that fictive world the physical environment, apart from Stone Court and Lowick Manor, are considerably less important than the carefully differentiated group of characters who help to unfold a typical view of pre-Victorian history, politics and law and an equally scrupulously researched estimate of the appropriate arts, sciences and scholarship of the early 1830s. They are also most deeply understood human beings made acquainted with failure even more than elated by success. To accommodate them Mr Purkis has most felicitously devised the emblem of a dinner table (p. 136) which is all the more delightful for having started out to be a redrawing of the web that is the term that George Eliot herself gives to the complexities of the society in her study of provincial England.

The volume bristles with helpful data and fresh ideas. The close study of representative passages of Eliot's prose that goes alongside the estimates of the novels as a whole seems to me most particularly valuable. Where else, though, can the reader turn for the whereabouts of a George Eliot Street or identify that view from a bridge (p. 163) that sustains and controls *The Mill on the Floss*?

MAURICE HUSSEY General Editor

Introduction

George Eliot's contemporaries had no doubt of her importance. She represented to the Victorians so many things which they admired—her apparently self-taught rise to intellectual eminence, her role as a translator of German theology, her special achievement as a new kind of novelist crowned by the Positivist *Romola*, and finally her faith in human beings and in the ultimate progress of the species. She was, as F. W. H. Myers said, one who 'did not despair of the Republic'. After a trough in her reputation, which lasted from her death until the nineteen-forties, she is now re-established as a great novelist, but increasingly associated with conservative rather than progressive values; *Middlemarch* is now seen as her supreme achievement, the kind of novel which all other novels aspire to become.

In writing about George Eliot I have tried to keep a balance between these attitudes. The first part of this book deals with aspects of her life, but I have deliberately departed from narrative in the second chapter in order to bring out the importance of the religious crisis; through that experience she came of age as a writer. The fourth chapter, too, is more abstract, and attempts to show how her doctrine of 'realism', used to test other novelists, led to her own experiments in writing fiction. The second part of the book is a critical survey of the novels, but only one is given extensive treatment; indeed, it could be said that I have tried to make all roads lead to *Middlemarch*. There are also a number of extracts from her works, intended to show the variety of her prose. Finally, the reference section makes a special point of linking the 'reality' in her novels to things which can still be seen today.

Even a slight acquaintance with George Eliot cannot fail to make the reader appreciate her courage and her stamina. I hope that anyone who feels inclined to pursue the translator of Strauss to earth, will simply get the book down from its usual resting-place, remote in the book-stack of a large library, and, in turning the pages, consider the scale of the enterprise involved in taking on such work. The labour of *Romola*, which she said aged her considerably, was another such undertaking; that book, however, is worth reading and I hope will soon regain its place as her great positive, as well as Positivist, novel.

With the republication of *Romola* in 1980 Penguin Books have completed the set of her novels for the general reader; Oxford are now making new library editions available. Scholarship smiles at the feast—'the missis has got one of her rare stuffed chines', as Mr

Poyser once indicated to Adam Bede. Life is short, and the reading of George Eliot's novels is one of its major experiences and pleasures. The purpose of this *Preface* is to try to encourage people to embark upon this venture, and, in the case of many readers, who already know some or all of the novels, to make links and connections between them. One needs to know something about George Eliot herself to appreciate both their serious moments and their jokes; as Gwendolen said in *Daniel Deronda*:

> Being acquainted with authors must give a peculiar understanding of their books: one would be able to tell then which parts were funny and which serious. I am sure I often laugh in the wrong place.

But then Gwendolen enjoyed teasing .... George Eliot, in spite of her reputation for seriousness, always knew how to make her readers laugh in the right place. I hope that this book will make her more easy to identify among 'the choir invisible'

Whose music is the gladness of the world.

List of abbreviations and standard references

George Eliot's novels are referred to by their full titles, and page references are those of the Penguin English Library editions.

Letters—*The George Eliot Letters* edited by Gordon S. Haight, published by Yale. Volumes 1–7 appeared in 1954–5; volumes 8 and 9 in 1978.

Essays—*Essays of George Eliot* edited by Thomas Pinney, published by Routledge and Kegan Paul, 1963.

Haight—*George Eliot: A Biography* by Gordon S. Haight, Oxford, 1968.

Part One
The Novelist in her Setting

Family tree of the Evans family

A note on names

Although we normally refer to her as George Eliot, this was a penname which Marian Evans adopted in 1857. In real life she was known by different names at different periods. She was christened Mary Anne, but this was soon altered to Mary Ann, both in her father's diaries and in her own usage from 1837. From 1850 she used Marian, perhaps as a result of her visit to Geneva, and allowed herself to be addressed as Polly or Pollian on some occasions.

After 1855 she began to call herself Mrs Lewes (pronounced Lewis), though she was not legally married to G. H. Lewes but had entered into 'a free union'. In 1880, after Lewes's death, she married John Walter Cross, and took his name as Mary Ann Cross.

Family tree of the Evans family

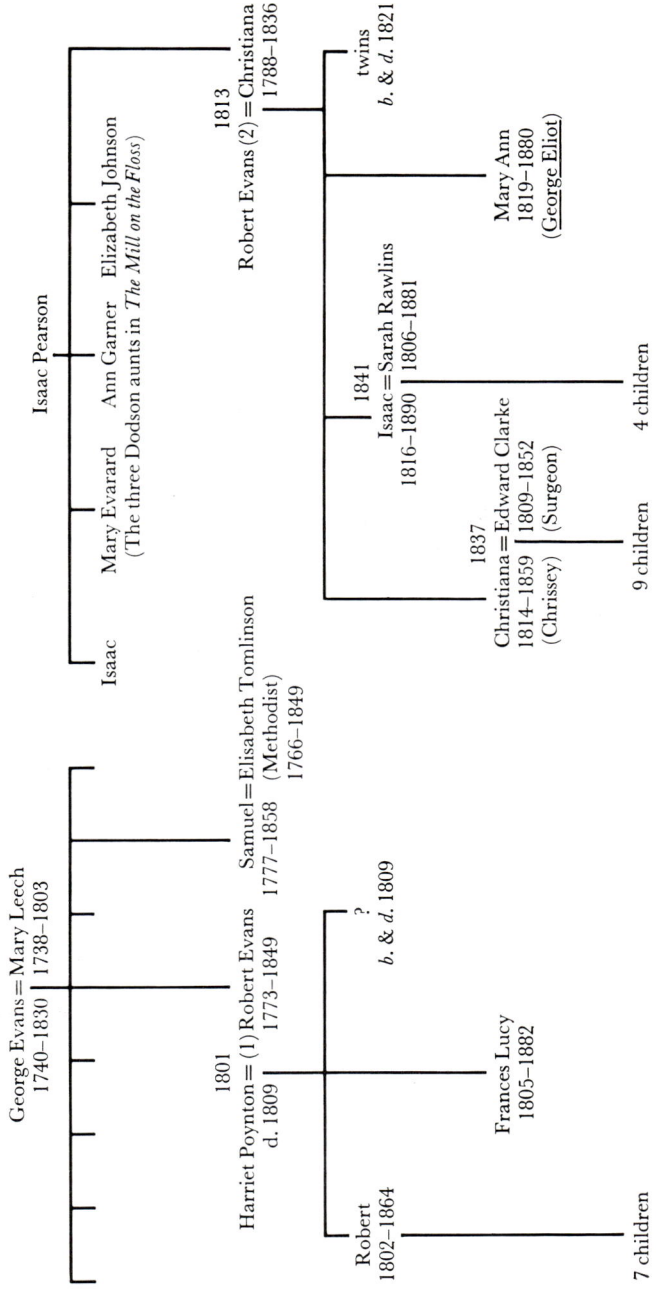

Chronological table

	GEORGE ELIOT'S LIFE	DATES RELEVANT TO HER WORKS
1773	Robert Evans born.	
1790		Setting of 'Mr Gilfil's Love Story'.
1799		Setting of *Adam Bede* is contemporary with her father's early manhood.
1819	(22 Nov.) Mary Anne Evans born at South Farm, Arbury, Warwickshire.	
1820	Her family move to Griff.	
1824	Attends dame-school; then to Miss Lathom's boarding-school at Attleborough.	Setting of *The Mill on the Floss* is contemporary with her own childhood.
1828	Moved to Mrs Wallington's school at Nuneaton; taught by Miss Maria Lewis.	Setting of 'Janet's Repentance'.
1829		Opening chapters of *Middlemarch* set at this time (further details on p. 123).
1830		Liverpool and Manchester railway begins to operate.
1832	Moved to the Misses Franklins' school at Warwick Row, Coventry.	(Feb.) First appearance of cholera in England. (May) Final pages of *Middlemarch*.

	(21 Dec.) Sees riot at Nuneaton on the occasion of the election of members for North Warwickshire; there was one fatality.	(7 June) Reform Bill passed. (1 Sep.) Opening of *Felix Holt*. (Dec.) Similar election riot in *Felix Holt*.
1836	(3 Feb.) Her mother dies.	
1837	(30 May) Her sister Christiana is married to Edward Clarke. Mary Ann becomes housekeeper to her father at Griff; he pays for her to be taught by visiting tutors.	
1838	Visits London with her brother Isaac.	
1839	Plans chart of Ecclesiastical History.	
1840		Poem published in the *Christian Observer*.
1841	Mary Ann and her father move to 21 Foleshill Road, Coventry. (8 June) Isaac marries Sarah Rawlins; he takes over Griff House. Mary Ann meets the Brays.	
1842	(2 Jan.) Mary Ann's refusal to attend church leads to a quarrel with her father. Reconciliation achieved in mid-May.	
1843	Visits the elderly scholar, Dr Brabant, at Devizes. Intensity of her devotion upsets his wife.	
1844		Begins to translate Strauss's *Das Leben Jesu*.

1845	(March) Engaged for a short time to a picture-restorer.	
1846		The translation is published as *The Life of Jesus critically examined*. Short essays published in the Coventry *Herald*.
1849	(31 May) Her father dies. (11 June) Mary Ann leaves for the Continent with the Brays; they leave her at Geneva for the winter.	
1850	(March) Returns to England; stays with relations and at the Brays. (18 Nov.) Stays at John Chapman's house in the Strand, London, for two weeks.	
1851	Again at Chapman's house for the first quarter of the year. After quarrels, she leaves for Coventry. (Sept.) Finally decides to return to Chapman's house. Becomes the unacknowledged 'editor' of the *Westminster Review*. At first her duties are menial, but she is soon commissioning and rewriting contributions. (Oct.) First meeting with G. H. Lewes.	Essay on 'The Progress of the Intellect' published in the *Westminster Review*.
1852	Friendship with Herbert Spencer. (July–Aug.) Visits Broadstairs.	

1853	(Oct.) Moves to 21 Cambridge St. Sees G. H. Lewes frequently.	Translates Feuerbach's *Das Wesen des Christentums*.
1854	(20 July) Leaves for Germany with G. H. Lewes, who is writing the life of Goethe.	The translation is published as *The Essence of Christianity*. Writes articles on Germany for the *Westminster Review*.
1855	(March) They return to England and after several changes of residence settle at Richmond in October.	Further essays and other journalism. Translates Spinoza's *Ethics* (never published).
1856	(May–Aug.) Visit to Ilfracombe and Tenby.	(23 Sep.) Begins to write fiction. (6 Nov.) Sends 'Amos Barton' to Blackwood, who accepts it.
1857	Summer visit to Scillies and Jersey. After the revelation of her 'marriage', Isaac and her family break with her.	'Amos' and the other early stories are serialised in *Blackwood's Magazine*; her authorship is concealed and the pseudonym of GEORGE ELIOT is adopted. (Oct.) Begins *Adam Bede*.
1858	(April–Aug.) Visit to Germany.	*Scenes of Clerical Life* published as a single book, in two volumes.
1859	Moves to Holly Lodge, Wandsworth. After other claims are made to the authorship of *Adam Bede*, she finally reveals who GEORGE ELIOT is. (Sep.) Visits Dorset, then Newark and Gainsborough for background to *The Mill on the Floss*.	*Adam Bede* published. Also 'The Lifted Veil'.
1860	(March–June) Visit to Italy: Rome, Naples, Florence. Interested in	*The Mill on the Floss* published.

	Savonarola. Returns via Switzerland.	
1861	Further visit to Florence; research into medieval period.	*Silas Marner* published.
1863	Profits from novels enable her to purchase The Priory, Regent's Park.	*Romola* published.
1864		'Brother Jacob' published.
1865	Difficulties in writing; abandons drama on Spanish subject.	
1866	(Dec.) Leaves for Spain.	*Felix Holt* published. Last major outbreak of cholera.
1867	(Mar) Returns from Spain. Summer visit to Germany.	Second Reform Act.
1868	Summer visit to Germany and Switzerland. (Sep.) Visit to Dr Allbutt at Leeds.	(Jan.) 'Address to Working Men by Felix Holt' in *Blackwood's*. *The Spanish Gypsy, a Poem* is published.
1869	Girton College founded. (March–May) Visit to Italy. Meets J. W. Cross at Rome. (19 Oct.) Thornton Lewes dies.	Begins *Middlemarch*.
1870		'The Legend of Jubal' (poem) published in *Macmillan's* magazine. Writes other poems during this period.
1871		(Dec.) First book of *Middlemarch* published.
1872		Remainder of *Middlemarch* published.

1873	(19–21 May) Visit to F. W. H. Myers at Cambridge. (June–Aug.) Visit to Germany; attends service at the Old Synagogue at Frankfurt.	
1874	First symptoms of stone in the kidney, which will be a recurrent illness.	*The Legend of Jubal and other Poems* published.
1875	Herbert Lewes dies in South Africa.	
1876	Buys country house at Witley.	*Daniel Deronda* published.
1877	Summer at Witley.	
1878	G. H. Lewes ill with cancer. (30 Nov.) G. H. Lewes dies.	
1879	Resolves to finish Lewes's *Problems of Life and Mind*. G. H. Lewes studentship created at Cambridge.	*Impressions of Theophrastus Such* (essays) published.
1880	Sees J. W. Cross frequently. (6 May) Marries J. W. Cross. Her brother Isaac writes to congratulate her. Honeymoon in Venice. (4 Dec.) Moves to 4 Cheyne Walk. (22 Dec.) Dies there. (29 Dec.) Buried in Highgate Cemetery.	
1885		J. W. Cross publishes *George Eliot's Life as Related in Her Letters and Journals*.

1 A provincial life

Robert Evans and his England

'... it's a fine thing to come to a man when he's seen into the nature of business; to have a chance of getting a bit of the country into good fettle, as they say, and putting men into the right way with their farming, and getting a bit of good contriving and solid building done — that those who are living and those who come after will be the better for. I'd sooner have it than a fortune. I hold it the most honourable work that is.' ...

'That it is, Caleb,' said his wife, with answering fervour. 'And it will be a blessing to your children to have had a father who did such work: a father whose good work remains though his name may be forgotten.'

Middlemarch, Ch. 40, p. 438

Not enough attention has been paid to George Eliot's father: Robert Evans demands not just a chapter but a book to himself.

Though the name Evans immediately suggests Welsh ancestry, the family had been established for several generations in the valley of the Dove, which divides Derbyshire from Staffordshire. Robert Evans was born in a small cottage, still to be seen, at Roston Common. At first he followed his father's trade of carpenter, and during his apprenticeship he learned all kinds of woodwork, including the manufacture of coffins; he received a rudimentary education in the village school, which was run by one Bartle Massey. (I mention these details because they were used by George Eliot in *Adam Bede*.) His affairs prospered, and he was able to move to a large house at Ellastone; because of his knowledge of timber he was employed as estate bailiff by a local landowner, Francis Parker of Wootton Hall. His first wife, Harriet Poynton, was also employed by the same family. In 1802 he moved with the Parker family to an estate which they had inherited at Kirk Hallam in Derbyshire, and again in 1806 to the Arbury Hall estate in North Warwickshire.

Francis Parker had to change his name to Newdigate on receiving this inheritance. The previous owner, Sir Robert Newdigate, who had died childless, was the last member of a family which had built up a concentration of land extending across five parishes. This process had gone on throughout the eighteenth century by

purchase and enclosure; Sir Robert had continued to extend his estate eastward, finally clinching the process by buying the disused colliery at Griff. Under proper management he knew this would yield enormous wealth if he could obtain access to the coal deposits beneath. A Newcomen engine was installed to pump out the workings, and a canal network constructed to convey the coal to the Coventry canal. From 1776 the reopened colliery began to produce returns on his investment, and some of the money was spent on the Gothic Revival additions to Arbury Hall.

Robert Evans was now the agent to the Parker Newdigate family, and the trusted manager of their Warwickshire estates; he carefully involved his brothers—and later his sons—in the business of management, placing them in positions from which he had 'moved on'. In Warwickshire he extended his own practice to include neighbouring estates; for example he worked roughly one day a week for Lord Aylesford at Great Packington. It is not entirely clear how he was paid, but he resided on one of the estate farms (Arbury Farm, now South Farm); though he was a tenant-farmer the rent was probably nominal; the records indicate that his colleague the mine steward paid £50 a year for a similar tenancy.

His first wife died in 1809; in 1813 he married into a local family of prosperous farmers. Christiana Pearson was considered to have demeaned herself by this marriage. The Pearsons can be fairly easily identified with the Dodsons in *The Mill on the Floss*; they were not 'peasants', and had a large amount of wealth in kind. The class system of rural England was clear and simple to those who inhabited it in those days, and probably lacked the finer points which have engrossed the attention of later historians. For country people there were really only three classes—the gentry or great landowners, their tenants who were middling farmers, and the labouring class which included the artisans. It was no simple matter to cross the gulfs which divided these classes; in economic terms they were clearly related to the ownership, the tenancy or the lack of land. Robert Evans, whose first marriage had been to another servant of the gentry, had to move geographically as well as socially before he was able to marry out of the class from which he had originally come.

Three children were born at Arbury Farm: Christiana in 1814, Isaac in 1816, and Mary Anne on 22 November 1819. Shortly after this event the family moved to Griff House, another estate property in the parish of Chilvers Coton. Though it was another farmhouse, it was close to the colliery at Griff and to the canal. Robert was strategically placed to keep an eye on these activities for his master; for example, it was his job to check the accounts. However, his major task lay on the surface of the land; he selected and vetted the

Robert Evans, by Carlisle, 1842

performance of the tenant-farmers of the estates under his control, and saw to the making of roads and the building of cottages.

We have a great deal of detailed information about these activities because Robert Evans kept a regular diary; not all the volumes have survived, but we have the series for 1830–2, for example. These are the years in which the events of *Middlemarch* are supposed to take place, though there is no evidence that the diaries were consulted by George Eliot during the preparations for her novel. What does emerge from the following carefully selected entries is a sense of the ambient reality from which certain passages in the novels must derive: these personal entries are comparatively rare, being surrounded by details of work done and lists of receipts or cash payments.

1830 Oct 28th	Mr & Mrs Johnson and Mr & Mrs Evarard & Mrs Hands came to tea with us	See family tree. Many entries like this can be compared to *The Mill on the Floss*, Bk I, Ch. 7.
1831 Jan 9th	I did not go to Church today Crissey & Mary Ann are both Ill in bed of the Measels.	One of the few occasions when the girls are mentioned.
Jan 10th	went to Hinckley new Market took Isaac with me in the Gig	Isaac on the other hand is being trained up to 'business' and goes out with his father when on holiday.
Aug 26th	Went to Thos Evans's property (?) at Kirkby with Brother Thos and my sons Robert & Isaac looked over his Farm. I had a new note Drawn up for £205 which he owed me and Thos Evans & his Father Signed it.	Refers to a holiday in Derbyshire without Mary Ann. Thos Evans does not appear to be a close relative, and he is distinguished from Brother Thos. This loan is like that in *The Mill on the Floss* Bk III, Chs 3 & 4, where the security is also a 'note'.
Aug 31st	went to Astley this morn at 4 oclock to see the Col. before he goes to London as he starts at 5	On return from his holiday he springs into activity. The Colonel is the son of his main

14

	oclock this morning, he Ordered a Double Cottage to be built at Nuthurst Heath, and a carthouse at Breach Oak Farm	employer; Robert Evans is the agent for both men. All these entries appear to refer to the same day.
	went to Dukes Farm ordered the Harvest Supper	
	went to Breach Oak Farm and Set out the carthouse	
	went with Smith and set out the Double Cottage	
	stopd at home all the afternoon making out my Accts etc	
	this day has cleared up well after a wet morning	
1832 Feb 4th	went to Nuneaton in the Afternoon took Mrs Evans with me. Settled with Mr Docker for Coals and paid him for Isaac's Schooling 5–13–0 Bt. of Mr. Morris 70 lb Kent Hops 4–7–6 Paid Mrs Wallington's Bill for Mary Ann's Schooling 23–3–0	If both payments for school fees are for the same period of time, then Isaac's 'schooling' is partly paid by barter.
Feb 12th	went to Coton Church in the forenoon. Mr. Gwyther Preached and Stopd the singers	See 'Amos Barton' Ch. 1 for details of the 'row' in church when this happened.

15

April 20th	went with Mrs. Evans to poor Isaac Pearsons Funieral I read the Will of his Father to them first and afterwards Isaac's Will Mr. Lovett was not pleased with Isaac's Will as he left all the stock to his Wife.	See extract p. 117. A Dodson must 'leave an unimpeachable will'. See *Middlemarch* Ch. 35 for the reading of Featherstone's will.
Nov 4th	this is a Butefull morning for the time of the year today is Coton Wakes Mr. Gwyther wishes to stop it on account of the Cholera being all round Us, being Affraid of people coming from places were they have had it and bringing it with them	The first mention of cholera in the diary. See *Middlemarch* p. 733. Robert represented his employers on the board of management of Bedworth Hospital, and though this was more an almshouse than a medical institution, it gives yet another link to the novel.

In addition to keeping his diaries, it was Robert Evans's duty to write weekly letters to his major employer, Francis Newdigate, who was frequently away in London. These letters are usually concerned with the business of the estate, but also give the local news. They reveal a rudimentary narrative gift in the writer which the spelling and punctuation may not have prepared us for. Some of the more interesting letters deal with embezzlement, fire and murder: in one case a plan of a cottage is attached. (See Appendix.)

The records indicate that Robert continued to administer the Arbury Hall estates until 1841, when he was sixty-eight. By then his wife had died, and he moved to Coventry with Mary Ann, leaving the newly married Isaac to take over Griff House and his father's job. But Robert continued to 'interfere', judging from surviving letters, until the middle of the 1840s. Mary Ann acted as his housekeeper until his death in 1849. From the chronological table it can be seen that Mary Ann spent half her life with her father, and his influence on her cannot be underestimated.

Robert Evans seems to have impressed everybody who knew him, either because of his physical strength or because of his sterling character. How he appeared to his own daughter is more of a problem; she knew him, in a sense, for thirty years, and he must have been a very dominating personality. A good deal can be inferred from reading her novels. For example, she must have listened to stories of his early life, and many aspects of the younger Robert Evans are idealised in the character of Adam Bede. Both are 'born' in the early 1770s; like Robert, Adam is trained as a carpenter, acquires a knowledge of timber, and eventually becomes master of his own business, besides having the buildings and general management of the Donithorne estate to attend to. The middle-aged Robert Evans, with his diverse activities, must contribute largely to the character of Caleb Garth in *Middlemarch*, though whether there is anything of Mrs Evans in Mrs Garth is impossible to determine, as we know so little about Mary Ann's mother; but the difficult times of 1835–6, when first Robert and then his wife became ill, are reflected in the illness and recovery of Mr Tulliver in *The Mill on the Floss*. Isaac seems to have temporarily taken over the work of the estate, which is echoed in the way in which Tom Tulliver, in spite of his expensive education, resolves to buckle down and assist his father.

The novelist also appears to receive from Robert Evans an attitude to manual labour which comes out again and again. After his father's sudden death Adam Bede does not have the time to lament; instead, he says:

> There's nothing but what's bearable as long as a man can work .... The square o' four is sixteen, and you must lengthen your lever in proportion to your weight, is as true when a man's miserable as when he's happy; and the best o' working is, it gives you a grip hold o' things outside your own lot.
>
> *Adam Bede*, Ch. 11, p. 160

Adam's involvement with his work is examined in some detail on pages 257–9 of Chapter 19—'Adam on a Working Day'. This is echoed by a similar long description of Caleb's attitude to 'myriad-headed, myriad-handed labour' in *Middlemarch* (Ch. 24, pp. 283–4), which rises at times to an equation of 'business' with poetry. These two characters impress us because they know their business; Adam Bede is a real carpenter who can make doors and coffins, and Caleb's general competence as an agent is often referred to. This belief in the worthwhile nature of hard work is genuinely held and not sentimentalised; a key to this is the scene where Caleb is approached by Fred Vincy, who wishes to learn Caleb's business instead of going into the Church. 'You must love your work,' says Caleb, '... and ... you must not be ashamed of your work.' (Ch. 56, p. 606)

The fact that work has an economic importance does not escape George Eliot's attention either. Lydgate needs to make money from his medical practice, or he will never be free from debt. In *The Mill on the Floss* we are never allowed to forget that the mill itself, and the right to draw off water, are the sources of the Tullivers' income; in *Adam Bede* the dairy where Hetty works is important because it enables the Poysers to live rather better than they would otherwise have done. Mary Ann knew about this because she had to oversee the dairy at Griff after her mother's death. And so George Eliot can write about these things from a point of view which is inside the class of skilled artisans, and convinces us that she knows how a tenant-farmer lived. This felt reality gives the novels their strength; even in *Silas Marner*, which is sometimes considered to be a kind of fairly tale, the figure of the weaver with his pack upon his back is drawn from observation: this was how the weavers of Stockingford appeared in her youth before the factory system was established.

From this concern with work, and the way in which work engages human beings with things outside themselves and with economic realities, there arises another quality in George Eliot's novels which goes back to the influence of her father. It is the way in which she perceives her task as a writer, and the way in which she undertakes to perform what she has promised to do. She is everything concerned with 'the solidity of objects'; in a difficult passage at the end of Chapter 21 of *Middlemarch*, page 243, she refers parenthetically to

> an idea wrought back to the directness of sense, like the solidity of objects.

This might be taken as a description of the process of writing, and also of the final impression; Henry James saw this concern with 'solidity' as her great virtue, and it is connected with her belief in realism, and her praise of Dutch painting—'the faithful representing of commonplace things'.

It is frequently observed that she writes best of her father's England. Her novels are usually set in the period before 1835, or even earlier; it is a world limited by horse-drawn transport, and the landscape is unchanged by the railways. The scenery is that of North Warwickshire; Birmingham and Stratford are over the horizon, and she is really only concerned with an area of about seven miles round Nuneaton and Coventry. The contrasted areas of Derbyshire and Staffordshire are connected with her father's past experiences. Socially, on the other hand, the range is wide; her father had access to people of all classes, so that Mary Ann knew what a baronet talked about in *Middlemarch*, and was able, in *Silas Marner*, to report the conversation in 'The Rainbow'. This world seems unshakable in its stability, though George Eliot and her readers knew that it had been overtaken by irreversible changes at the time when she presented it to them.

Finally, although she was to become famous as a liberal and progressive writer, her novels contain in addition a backward-looking tendency which seems to doubt the wisdom of precipitate change. At the end of her life she wrote some essays under the pseudonym of Theophrastus Such; in one of these she explains that her

> father was a Tory who had not exactly a dislike to innovators and dissenters, but a slight opinion of them as persons of illfounded self-confidence.... certain conservative prepossessions have mingled themselves for me with the influence of our Midland scenery.
>
> 'Looking Backward'

That is to say that the voice which she had heard so many times in her youth decrying new-fangled ideas never ceased to blend itself with her work, and contributed, for example, to the unspoken dialogue which enlivens the first page of her fiction (Shepperton Church), where the imagination delights in 'a little Toryism by the sly' (see p. 90). But all this has brought us to a point a long way ahead in our story; it is time to look more closely at the education which Robert Evans provided for his daughter, and how it led to a violent disagreement between them.

Childhood and schooltime

> 'a woman's no business wi' being so clever; it'll turn to trouble, I doubt. But, bless you!' — here the exultation was clearly recovering the mastery — 'she'll read the books and understand 'em, better nor half the folks as are growed up.'
>
> Mr Tulliver in *The Mill on the Floss*, Bk I, Ch. 3, p. 66

George Eliot's earliest memories were of her brother Isaac, whom she followed everywhere, worshipping him for his strength and his decisiveness, and terrified lest she should fall out of his favour; he, on the other hand, was responsible for seeing that she didn't fall into 'our brown canal'. For evidence of this period of her life we have to rely on the 'Brother and Sister' sonnets, published in 1874, and the anecdotes related in the early chapters of *The Mill on the Floss*: Tom and Maggie are born in the same years as Isaac and Mary Ann, and it is usually assumed that the neat and tidy Lucy resembles her sister Chrissey. But *The Mill on the Floss* is not really evidence, and is steeped in the emotions of regret and remorse which must be discounted in trying to arrive at a true picture of the young Mary Ann.

After attending a dame-school she was sent to a boarding-school in a nearby village at the age of five. This may seem strange, but social customs vary from generation to generation, and in any case her mother may not have been able to cope. (Haight suggests that she was already in a poor state of health.) At nine Mary Ann was moved to Miss Wallington's establishment in Nuneaton: this was a Church of England school with thirty boarders. The child was considered to be 'clever', and came under the influence of a teacher called Miss Maria Lewis, an earnest Evangelical (see p. 27ff.). Finally, her father sent her to a much larger boarding-school, the Misses Franklins' at Coventry, where she was taught to drop the local dialect and accent, exchanging them for an exceptionally compelling 'low voice' in imitation of one of her teachers.

The Franklins' school is obviously the crucial one in Mary Ann's development, and deserves some tentative speculation on our part. In the first place, it should not be confused with Miss Lemon's Academy in the town of Middlemarch, where Rosamond Vincy finished her education. Of course the parents would expect the girls to be taught French, music and sketching, that is 'the accomplishments', as in Jane Austen's day, but there is some evidence that the pupils were occasionally exposed to ideas. One of Mary Ann's exercise books of 1834 has survived, containing an essay and a fragment of a novel (see Haight's Appendix); these provide ample testimony to the quality of the English teaching at the school. The father of the two Miss Franklins, the Reverend Francis Franklin, was a Baptist minister: he is traditionally assumed to be the original of the character of Rufus Lyon in *Felix Holt*: the undoubted scope of his intellect, shown in the sermons he preached in his chapel in Cow Lane, seems to have contributed to Mary Ann's reverence for things of the mind. On the other hand, we cannot describe this school as a Dissenting Academy: it was an institution from which most girls would move on to an early marriage.

At this point the expectations of her father and her family must be brought into consideration. It is usually assumed that in this period of history all the family's attention would have been focused on the boy, but in fact Isaac fared worse than Mary Ann in his education. He was sent to Mr Docker, a private tutor in Birmingham; there is a short 'essay' about the luck of the draw in education on page 241 of *The Mill on the Floss* which rings true. In choosing schools for his children the father seems to have tried to buy status, but he was not influenced by religious prejudices, since the boy was exposed to High Church influence, while the girl was handed over to Evangelical and Nonconformist teachers. It may be argued that Robert Evans was not interested in religious differences, and took his religion from his employers, but even so, the change *from* an Anglican to a Nonconformist establishment is very broadminded for the time, and adds to the case that the father did want to do the best he could for his clever daughter.

After all, Robert Evans, for all his gifts of character and application, had not learned to spell at Bartle Massey's, except 'on an impromptu phonetic system' like Mr Tulliver's (*The Mill on the Floss* p. 241). The embarrassment of this may well have made him want more for his children than he had obtained himself. Nevertheless, Isaac, in spite of his superior education, was not expected to go beyond his father: he succeeded him as manager of the Arbury estates, and spent the rest of his life in the same job. It is no surprise, therefore, that Mary Ann's expectations were, in the first instance, no more than to replace her mother; when Mrs Evans died Mary Ann does not seem to have raised any objection to becoming housekeeper at Griff.

Yet we still have not explained how a country child of no particular advantages could become an intellectual prodigy. Perhaps the explanation is not to be found in the schools at all, and without claiming that the novelist George Eliot was the end result of Mary Ann Evans's self-taught 'genius', we should pay some attention to her early reading and private study. The Evangelical poetry which she admired in these years is uniformly banal, but on the other hand the Evangelical training made her study the Bible and practise self-examination. In spite of her later exclamations to Miss Maria Lewis about novel-reading (see p. 59), she read Sir Walter Scott and his imitators from an early age; there do not seem to have been any restrictions upon novel reading in her schools, and later on—in her twenties—she had to read Scott every night to her ailing father. While, at that time, historical novels were regarded as light entertainment, she learned a great deal from Scott; apart from giving her an insight into the strategies of fiction—he is very good at organising apparently unrelated materials into a whole work—he transcended the limitations of her provincial world. He introduced her to romantic legends, far-away countries, and distant times. The sweep of his imagination opened wider vistas than the narrow outlook of Bible-based religion. Most important was his sense of historical development; in later years she said that perhaps her loss of faith was caused by reading Scott, and from his love of the Scottish peasantry we can trace her enthusiasm for the social theories of von Riehl (see p. 83).

To sum up, it is very easy to think of North Warwickshire in the 1830s as too small a world to nourish such a writer as George Eliot, but we must not forget that even before the railway age, as we can see from the roughly contemporary childhood of the Brontës, the books, magazines and reviews of the time had an extensive circulation, and rapidly disseminated new ideas to even the remotest parts of the kingdom.

Intellectual awakening

> 'I do not believe it!' said Romola, her whole frame shaken with passionate repugnance, 'God's kingdom is something wider—else, let me stand outside it with the beings that I love.'
>
> *Romola*, Ch. 59, p. 578

After her mother's death in 1836 and her sister's marriage in 1837, Mary Ann was left at home in full charge of the domestic arrangements; of course there were servants, but she did get involved in messy things like jam-making. Her father encouraged her intellectual ambitions by paying for private tutors to visit the house; their fees seem quite expensive for the time. There were lessons for several years in Italian, German and Latin. In addition her father allowed her to buy as many books as she needed, and she was able to keep up with new publications by ordering them when they first appeared as part-works. She was allowed to use the library at Arbury Hall, described by Haight as 'a great library ... which had been growing steadily since Queen Elizabeth's day.' But it can be seen from the surviving correspondence that it was *social* life that she lacked, though friends and former teachers came to stay.

The years between 1836 and 1841 seem to have been very important in Mary Ann's intellectual development, after one has acknowledged the obvious truism that the years between sixteen and twenty-two are important for everybody's mental growth. In Mary Ann's case three strands in this development are worth following up.

In the first place, her social conscience seems to have been aroused. During a period of economic distress in the surrounding villages, she was not content with the usual charitable activities such as church bazaars, and took a further practical step: she 'organised a clothing club for the families of unemployed ribbon weavers' (Haight p. 26). This is a foretaste of how, in *Middlemarch*, Dorothea desired to be useful 'among the cottagers'.

Secondly, she developed a more serious interest in poetry. At this period in her life she read the principal Romantic poets; in 1839 she bought a six-volume Wordsworth—'I never before met with so many of my own feelings, expressed just as I could like them' (*Letters*, I 54). In fact Wordsworth's influence was life-long, and will be discussed in the section on 'Wordsworth and the power of memory' (p. 65). His views on the beneficent influence of Nature were at last being treated seriously; the 1830s and 40s are 'the Age of Wordsworth', and his disciples, such as Emerson, were trying to propagate a new 'religion' of Transcendentalism. Wordsworth opened her mind to alternative beliefs to those of Evangelicalism, though she still clung to her religion with gloomy persistence at this time; it is worth noting that later, during the 1840s, she developed a kind of Pantheism as a substitute for Christianity.

Finally, she decided to investigate the records of the early Church, in order to draw up a chart of Ecclesiastical History. She described this plan in a letter to Maria Lewis:

> I will just (if you can bear to hear more of the matter) give you an idea of the plan, which may have partly faded from your memory. The series of perpendicular columns will successively contain, the Roman Emperors with their dates, the political and religious state of the Jews, the bishops, remarkable men and events in the several churches, a column being devoted to each of the chief ones, the aspect of heathenism and Judaism toward Christianity, the chronology of the Apos [tolical] and Patristical writings, schisms and heresies, General Councils, eras of corruption, under which head the remarks would be general, and I thought possibly an application of the Apocalyptic prophecies, which would merely require a few figures and not take up room. I think there must be a break in the chart after the establishment of Christianity as the religion of the Empire, and I have come to a determination not to carry it beyond the first acknowledgment of the supremacy of the Pope, by Phocas in 606 when Mohammedanism became a besom of destruction in the hand of the Lord, and completely altered the aspect of Ecclesiastical Hist[or]y. So much for this, at present, airy project, about which I hope never to teaze you more.
>
> *Letters*, I 44–5, 30 March 1840

These studies led her to consider the origins of Christianity; in Isaac Taylor's *Ancient Christianity*, which she read at this time, she was disturbed to find accounts of corruption, even in the early Church.

When Robert Evans retired in 1841, he moved to Coventry with Mary Ann. They established themselves in a large suburban house in the Foleshill Road; it was called 'Bird Grove' (see p. 168). This sham rurality may not have deceived Robert Evans, who would have preferred to live in a country cottage; the real reason for the move was to get Mary Ann into society for the usual purpose— marriage. What in fact happened was that she was thrown into the company of Charles Bray, a ribbon manufacturer of advanced views and relaxed attitudes; he and Mary Ann were observed walking 'arm in arm like lovers'. Bray was a writer on phrenology and educational subjects; phrenology will be discussed later, but at this time it was a rallying-point for the intellectual *avant-garde*. Bray was in fact an atheist; he had married a Unitarian, Caroline Hennell, who was extremely worried by her husband's irreverence. She therefore asked her brother Charles to help her.

In response to her request Charles Hennell had made a thorough study of the evidence, and in 1838 had published *An Inquiry into the Origins of Christianity*; he examined the Scriptures as if they were any other book, and concluded that Christianity was not the result of supernatural but of real causes and events. He decided that Christ was a man, but his followers were genuine in their supernatural beliefs because they were writing under the influence of the mythology prevalent at the time. Though this method of approaching the Bible and its conclusions have become familiar as the 'German Higher Criticism' (see the section on Strauss and Feuerbach pp. 39–45), it is worth pointing out that Hennell himself was unaware of German scholarship and had worked all this out for himself. His book was, of course, a confirmation of Charles Bray's position, and of no use to Caroline.

Mary Ann was therefore, as it were, called in as a messenger of the Gospel; she was supposed to bring the light of Evangelicalism to the benighted Brays. In fact, the reverse occurred; she began to devour Hennell's *Inquiry*, and was presumably exposed to the arguments of Charles Bray's new book, *The Philosophy of Necessity*— 'mind is subject to fixed laws such as matter is.' This brought on a crisis, which is elliptically described in Robert Evans's Journal:

> January 2. Went to Trinity Church in the forenoon. Miss Lewis went with me. Mary Ann did not go. I stopd the sacrament and Miss Lewis stopd also.
>
> January 14. Miss Lewis is here and she is waiting to go by the Mail to Nuneaton to take possession of her new school at Nuneaton.
>
> January 16. went to church in the forenoon Mary Ann did not go to church.

She did not go the next week either, and this led to a situation which she called her 'Holy War'. She felt that she could not speak to her father, and after nine weeks decided to write him a letter:

> Foleshill Monday Morning.
>
> My dear Father,
>
> As all my efforts in conversation have hitherto failed in making you aware of the real nature of my sentiments, I am induced to try if I can express myself more clearly on paper so that both I in writing and you in reading may have our judgements unobstructed by feeling, which they can hardly be when we are together. I wish entirely to remove from your mind the false notion that I am inclined visibly to unite myself with any Christian community, or that I have any affinity in opinion with Unitarians more than with other classes of believers in the Divine authority of the books comprising the Jewish and Christian Scriptures. I regard these writings as histories consisting of mingled

truth and fiction, and while I admire and cherish much of what I believe to have been the moral teaching of Jesus himself, I consider the system of doctrines built upon the facts of his life and drawn as to its materials from Jewish notions to be most dishonourable to God and most pernicious in its influence on individual and social happiness. In thus viewing this important subject I am in unison with some of the finest minds in Christendom in past ages, and with the majority of such in the present (as an instance more familiar to you than any I could name I may mention Dr. Franklin). Such being my very strong convictions, it cannot be a question with any mind of strict integrity, whatever judgement may be passed on their truth, that I could not without vile hypocrisy and a miserable truckling to the smile of the world for the sake of my supposed interests, profess to join in worship which I wholly disapprove. This and *this alone* I will not do even for your sake—anything else however painful I would cheerfully brave to give you a moment's joy.

I do not hope to convince any other member of our family and probably not yourself that I am really sincere, that my only desire is to walk in that path of rectitude which however rugged is the only path to peace, but the prospect of contempt and rejection shall not make me swerve from my determination so much as a hair's breadth until I feel that I *ought* to do so. From what my Brother more than insinuated and from what you have yourself intimated I perceive that your establishment at Foleshill is regarded as an unnecessary expense having no other object than to give me a centre in society—that since you now consider me to have placed an insurmountable barrier to my prosperity in life this one object of an expenditure held by the rest of the family to be disadvantageous to them is frustrated—I am glad at any rate this is made clear to me, for I could not be happy to remain as an incubus or an unjust absorber of your hardly earned gains which might be better applied among my Brothers and Sisters with their children.

I should be just as happy living with you at your cottage at Packington or any where else if I can thereby minister in the least to your comfort—of course unless that were the case I must prefer to rely on my own energies and resources feeble as they are—I fear nothing but voluntarily leaving you. I can cheerfully do it if you desire it and shall go with deep gratitude for all the tenderness and rich kindness you have never been tired of shewing me. So far from complaining I shall joyfully submit if as a proper punishment for the pain I have most unintentionally given you, you determine to appropriate any provision you may have intended to make for my future support to your other children whom you may consider more deserving. As a last vindication of herself from one who has no one to speak for her I may be permitted to say that if ever I loved you I do so now, if ever I sought to obey the laws of my Creator and to follow duty wherever it may lead me I have that determination now and the consciousness of this will support me though every being on earth were to frown upon me.

> Your affectionate Daughter
> Mary Ann.
> *Letters*, I 128–30

Her father's response was to put the house up for sale.

Finally, thanks to the interposition of friends and relations, a compromise was reached. Mary Ann would attend church in future, but she would think what she liked. Robert Evans's Journal contains the short but significant entry:

May 14th   Went to Trinity Church. Mary Ann went with me.

The reconciliation lasted, and Mary Ann continued to look after her father until his death in 1849. But her mind was drawn into a wider world; she entered into religious controversies in order to settle her own beliefs, and then took part, an active partisan, in contributing to the liberal side of the debate.

2 The religious crisis of the nineteenth century

Doubts and difficulties

> Probably no English writer of the time, and certainly no novelist, more fully epitomizes the century; her development is a paradigm, her intellectual biography a graph, of its most decided trend. Starting from Evangelical Christianity, the curve passes through doubt to a reinterpreted Christ and a religion of humanity: beginning with God, it ends in Duty.
>
> Basil Willey, Nineteenth Century Studies

Disputes about religion such as that between Mary Ann and her father may seem comical in retrospect; normally neither side can be persuaded to yield an inch. In this more general chapter the importance of religious belief as a thing *in itself* worth quarrelling over is assumed; but it seems that at certain times a quarrel which is apparently about religion may really be about something quite different. For example, it may be about the need to hold society together (everybody should go to the same Church as the ruler of the country), about who shall be the master (Pope or King), or about control of the Church at a local level (bishops or laity); these are ancient history. More modern instances can be interpreted as divisions between classes (the Church of England against the Nonconformists), about nationalism (the rôle of the Catholic Church in Ireland or Poland), or about feminism (women as priests). At a more general crisis of religious history, such as the Reformation, everything may be called in question: we seem to be witnessing one of those periodic upheavals in the world of ideas when a total system of thought, which its adherents are so controlled by that they are unable to imagine any alternative, is overthrown and replaced by another. Mary Ann's personal difficulties can only be understood as part of another such general crisis.

Though the process was long drawn out, doubts and difficulties in religion became a matter of acute concern in the 1830s and 40s. In the first place, the institution of religion embodied in the Church of England was under attack from both flanks. On the one hand, there was the attempt by the Evangelicals to take over the Church from within. Though the Evangelical Movement was eighteenth century in origin, and attempted to call people back to the 'seriousness' of their Christian beliefs, it had gained ground during the period of the Napoleonic Wars, when a literal belief in the Bible, and a simplified view of the righteousness of their cause, must have seemed one way of rebutting the ideas generated by the French Revolution. Led by William Wilberforce and Charles Simeon, Evangelicalism infiltrated the Church of England by making converts among the ruling classes. It was a peculiarly English movement, and its strength lay in its extremely limited vision of the world.

On the other hand, the emancipation of the Catholics (1829) seemed far more of a threat to the national Church, because it undermined the unique authority of the Church of England. Such change had not seemed possible, and was followed in 1832 by the passing of the great Reform Bill, which, whatever its actual provisions, made it clear that the future lay with popular forces who saw the Church of England as an irrelevance. (It is no accident that George Eliot chooses this period for the setting of two of her novels.) This shaking of the established basis of English society produced reactions in its turn. For example, John Henry Newman saw the need to reaffirm the authority of the Church by asserting its Catholic origins: the son of an Evangelical mother, he too looked for certainties and clear solutions. Ultimately, having led the Oxford or High Church Movement for many years, he joined the Roman Catholic Church, so confirming the suspicions of his enemies.

At a time of national crisis, the pressures on individuals were intense and overwhelming; endless debate led some people to doubt all religious certainties. The Church, the Bible, and even God himself were rejected; new ideas in theology and science all contributed to an intellectual renaissance, coupled with a sense of bleakness and despair at the loss of personal immortality. For example, Tennyson's *In Memoriam*, in its most deeply felt passages, shows a mind profoundly disturbed by the new discoveries in embryology and in geology; the book was published in 1850 but contains verses from the previous eighteen years. George Eliot did not record her crisis in this way, and in this chapter we need to look carefully at the different stages of her beliefs, examining both what she rejects and what she builds in its place.

Church and chapels

> many of us can remember country districts in which the great mass of the people were christianised by illiterate Methodist and Independent ministers, while the influence of the parish clergyman among the poor did not extend much beyond a few old women in scarlet cloaks, and a few exceptional church-going labourers.
>
> 'The Natural History of German Life'

In this section we look back over George Eliot's youth, noticing the varieties of religious experience which came her way, and at the same time observing how these differ one from another. Though these differences would have been a matter of hot debate to her at her most impressionable age, in her middle years they have become coolly translated into the materials of her fiction. The various sects, and the social peculiarities of their adherents, will be regarded from outside by a novelist who has gone through this particular fire, and understands the meaning of the scars she bears. She has become, as far as the issues are concerned, a detached observer, yet in the contemplation of those issues she recreates, in one or other of her characters, a version of her own youthful involvement.

Mary Ann Evans had been baptised into the Church of England by the Reverend Bernard Gilpin Ebdell, Vicar of Chilvers Coton and Astley from 1786 to 1828. As she grew up Mary Ann would have met many examples of similar 'eighteenth century clergymen'; they had survived from a time when the fundamentals of religion were not a subject for controversy, though they sincerely believed that their mission was to regulate social behaviour. The churchmen of this generation are epitomised in the unfortunate Mr Gilfil, who is the subject of the second of the *Scenes of Clerical Life*; his name is Ebdell's in a disguised form. In carrying out his duties he relied on a batch of yellowing sermons which dealt with everyday morality and worked 'by repetition'. A later example of the same kind of cleric is Mr Farebrother in *Middlemarch*; his acute mind is divided between genuine scientific interests and remunerative cardplaying. But the type is epitomised in the incomparable Mr Irwine of *Adam Bede*, a novel which is set in the last years of the eighteenth century; of Mr Irwine a contemporary (1859) lady reader might have said—or so George Eliot informs us—'This rector of Broxton is little better than a pagan!' (p. 221). Indeed, the whole of Chapter 17 of *Adam Bede* could be extracted and read as a most pertinent introduction to the subject under discussion; in the lady reader George Eliot is guying her own younger self. By 1859 she was kinder and more tolerant towards these elder representatives of the Church of England: she has learnt to appreciate their ethical wisdom, and can joke about them because she has come to respect their wide humanity.

Evangelicalism she met at school in Nuneaton. In contrast to the gentler correction practised by the older clergy, it was intolerant of opposition in deed or thought. Its practitioners were quietly fanatical, and they were not restricted to the clergy. Like most Protestant sects, it inclined towards the priesthood of all believers'; the responsibilities of each individual soul were onerous and could not be ignored. Its adherents gave to every tiny moral decision eternal value, whether such decisions actually entered into life or were simply a form of mental gymnastics; reading the early letters of Mary Ann we find her desperately seeking for things to feel guilty about. One action can lead to another, so that one was taught to explore the consequences of each action thoroughly; on it might depend one's hopes of Heaven or Hell. The influence of these doctrines on Mary Ann can be said to date from 1828, when she met Miss Lewis, the same year in which Mr Edmund Jones began to preach in Nuneaton. The doctrines of 'serious' Christianity had taken a long time to arrive in that town; for their reception there, look at the third story, 'Janet's Repentance', in *Scenes of Clerical Life*, where Mr Jones is portrayed as Mr Tryan. Mary Ann wrote many letters to Maria Lewis in which the severer mortifications are discussed: for example, we learn that oratorios are 'not consistent with millennial holiness' (*Letters*, I 9).

These gloomy tendencies were encouraged by the Calvinism which she imbibed at the Misses Franklins': 'I feel myself a mere cumberer of the ground' (*Letters*, I 12). But by 1840 she had begun to lose her Evangelical certainties, and in later life was critical of her former self— 'I used to go about like an owl.' Finally, in 1855, in her article on 'Evangelical Teaching', she slaughtered the unfortunate Dr Cumming, a famous preacher, together with the beliefs she had once shared with him. Nevertheless, in her novels, which of course postdate this essay, the Evangelicals are portrayed ambiguously: in 'Janet's Repentance' there is a long passage describing the *good* which Evangelicalism had brought to Milby (Nuneaton)— 'that recognition of something to be lived for beyond the mere satisfaction of self' (pp. 320–1). Against this we learn in *Middlemarch* that the Vincy's house was a merry one at a 'time when Evangelicalism had cast a certain suspicion as of plague-infection over the few amusements which survived in the provinces' (p. 191). In the same novel its adherents are portrayed as narrow and self-seeking: a good deal of attention is given to Mr Bulstrode and his 'serious' Christian beliefs (pp. 156–9). When Dorothea has to decide who is to have the living at Lowick (pp. 536–8), the candidates are Mr Tyke 'the Apostolic man', who is Bulstrode's nominee, and Mr Farebrother; it is interesting to see that she rejects Tyke not because he is low class, but because he is above the heads of ordinary people—'I cling to that which is truest—I mean that which takes in the most good of all kinds, and brings in the most people as sharers in it. It is surely better to pardon too much, than to condemn too much.' So she gives the living to Farebrother, and I think that the reader is meant to feel—out in the world beyond the pages of the novel—that this is George Eliot's as well as Dorothea's choice.

Whereas the Evangelicals stressed the importance of the individual soul, the Oxford Movement emphasised the claims of the

Church. Isaac Evans was exposed to High Church influence from Mr Docker in Birmingham, and Maggie, in *The Mill on the Floss*, reads the Catholic mystic Thomas à Kempis and puts her trust in Dr Ken; but one could be forgiven for not seeing Maggie as particularly High Church. In *Scenes of Clerical Life* Amos Barton, whose 'Christian experience had been consolidated at Cambridge under the influence of Mr Simeon' (p. 67) and whom we therefore expect to see as an Evangelical, nevertheless seems to have combined his Low Church preaching with a High Church assertion of clerical powers (p. 53). The signals are confusing; one would go to another novelist such as Charlotte Yonge for a real understanding of this movement. It was not something of which George Eliot had any experience or which she was likely to regard with sympathy.

With Nonconformity, on the other hand, she was quite at home, though in theory the gulf between Church and Chapel was immense. Historically the division went back to the Civil War of the seventeenth century and the ensuing legislation: the Nonconformists were socially and ideologically a separate nation, Dissent, and had been penalised politically and educationally. In practice, however, these disadvantages frequently led to advantage. For example, the Nonconformists took good care that their educational system should be second to none, and we have seen that Mary Ann attended a school run by Baptists in Coventry.

In the eighteenth century there had been a religious revival. The preaching of Wesley led to the founding of the Methodist Church, and to the revitalisation of other sects. This affected the Evans family, so that whatever we may think of the conforming religion of Mary Ann's father, we must bear in mind that one of his brothers became a Baptist and two became Methodists. The fortunes of Samuel Evans and his wife are worth following in detail (see 'Brief biographies' in Part Three). Mary Ann corresponded with her aunt, and they exchanged visits in the years 1839–42. It is no wonder that when she came to write *Adam Bede* George Eliot's view of Methodism was so positive:

> this blessed gift of venerating love has been given to too many humble craftsmen since the world began, for us to feel any surprise that it should have existed in the soul of a Methodist carpenter half a century ago, while there was yet a lingering after-glow from the time when Wesley and his fellow-labourer fed on the hips and haws of the Cornwall hedges, after exhausting limbs and lungs in carrying a divine message to the poor.
>
> That after-glow has long faded away; and the picture we are apt to make of Methodism in our imagination is not an amphitheatre of green hills, or the deep shade of broad-leaved sycamores, where a crowd of rough men and weary-hearted

Dinah Morris Preaching on the Green *by Edward Henry Corbould, see Adam Bede, Chapter 2.*

women drank in a faith which was a rudimentary culture, which linked their thoughts with the past, lifted their imagination above the sordid details of their own narrow lives, and suffused their souls with the sense of a pitying, loving, infinite Presence, sweet as summer to the houseless needy. It is too possible that to some of my readers Methodism may mean nothing more than low-pitched gables up dingy streets, sleek grocers, sponging preachers and hypocritical jargon—elements which are regarded as an exhaustive analysis of Methodism in many fashionable quarters.

That would be a pity; for I cannot pretend that Seth and Dinah were anything else than Methodists—not indeed of that modern type which reads quarterly reviews and attends in chapels with pillared porticoes; but of a very old-fashioned kind. They believed in present miracles, in instantaneous conversions, in revelations by dreams and visions; they drew lots, and sought for Divine guidance by opening the Bible at hazard; having a literal way of interpreting the Scriptures, which is not at all sanctioned by approved commentators; and it is impossible for me to represent their diction as correct, or their instruction as liberal.

Adam Bede, Ch. 3, p. 82

The less pleasant aspects of Nonconformity appear in *Silas Marner* and *Middlemarch*. When Silas said 'I've never been to church' (p. 137), he strikes amazement into the heart of good Dolly Winthrop: living in a rural parish she cannot comprehend his notion of 'chapel', the place where he worshipped in an industrial town. Silas's chapel seems to have been a survival of early Nonconformity, though it contains within it the same practices referred to in the extract cited from *Adam Bede*, such as seeking guidance from the Bible and the strange ceremony of drawing lots to determine guilt. Nevertheless, there is a perception of the place assigned to Nonconformity in the urban community, and there is a special vividness in the description of 'the Church assembling in Lantern Yard.' Marner eventually learns to attend church as part of his incorporation into the society of his village; we are not made to feel this is insincere. Brother Bulstrode, on the other hand, who had grown up in a similar environment— 'an eminent young member of a Calvinistic dissenting church at Highbury' (*Middlemarch* p. 663)—found that his ambition led him to embrace the Church of England, or at any rate the Low Church wing of it. 'Still in the Dissenting line, eh?' asks his old friend Raffles, 'Still godly? Or taken to the Church as more genteel?' (p. 572)

Finally, a special mention must be made of the Unitarians, a small and select group of families, whose tradition of anti-

Trinitarianism went back to the seventeenth century. By this time they were the leading intellectual Nonconformist society. The Hennells were a Unitarian family, and Mary Ann clung to Sara Hennell and Cara Bray for support and understanding after she had 'lost her faith'. Though she did not join their sect, she kept in touch with them; in 1880, whatever her private beliefs may have amounted to, she was buried according to the Unitarian rite.

Summing up, we may note that even though, from 1850 onwards, she was to be associated with the public dissemination and propagandising of liberal ideas through the *Westminster Review*, her wide experience of the inner and the outer world of Christianity remained with her: in particular, many of the self-questionings and soul-searchings of her early Evangelical training stayed with her always. No action was too trivial, no person too insignificant for her to consider and weigh. Though the connection may seem obscure, these preoccupations were reinforced by phrenology and the deterministic beliefs to which she was exposed at the Brays, and which deserve more consideration than is usually given to them.

Phrenology

> Mr Letherall was a large man in spectacles, who one day took my small head between his large hands, and pressed it here and there in an exploratory, suspicious manner—then placed each of his great thumbs on my temples, and pushed me a little away from him, and stared at me with glittering spectacles. The contemplation appeared to displease him, for he frowned sternly, and said to my father, drawing his thumbs across my eyebrows—
>
> 'The deficiency is there, sir—there; and here,' he added, touching the upper sides of my head, 'here is the excess. That must be brought out, sir, and this must be laid to sleep.'
>
> 'The Lifted Veil'

Whereas some Victorian images or ideas still have a meaning for twentieth-century contemplation—the valentine, the Christmas card, the locomotive or the vampire, to name but a few—this white and labelled head seems as remote as a Babylonian tablet or an Aztec temple. Phrenology has completely disappeared from our view of the world, and must be one of the few discredited ideas that did not undergo a revival in the nineteen sixties. Its successors, on the one hand behaviourism, and on the other hand Freudian psychology, continue to flourish, and are regarded by many people as scientific accounts of the human mind.

It requires a considerable effort of the imagination to see that phrenology was, if anything, the conclusion of a chain of reasoning which seemed unassailable. If there are no supernatural forces or spirits which could account for mental phenomena, then the mind

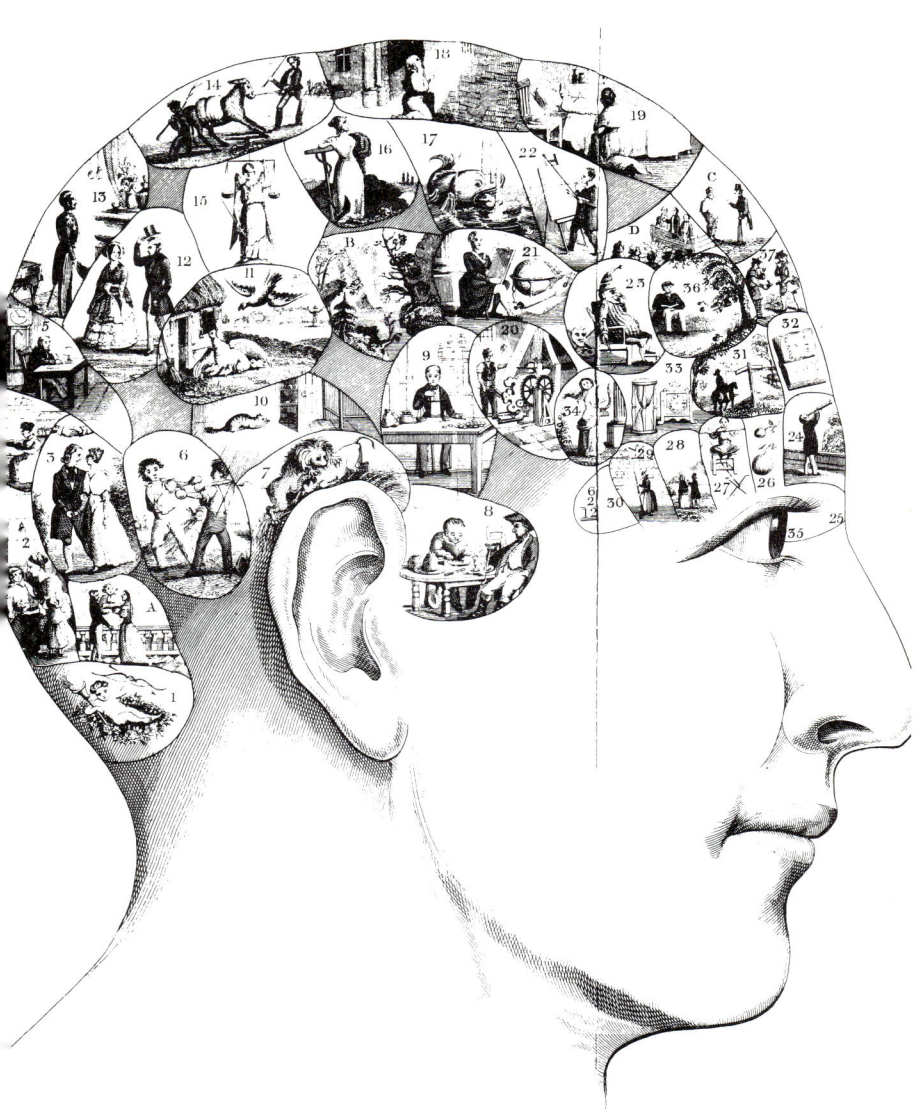

KEY TO SYMBOLICAL HEAD.

mativeness.	9. Acquisitiveness.	17. Marvellousness.	25. Form. 26. Size.	34. Tune.
hiloprogenitiveness.	10. Secretiveness.	18. Veneration.	27. Weight.	35. Language.
dhesiveness.	11. Cautiousness.	19. Benevolence.	28. Colour.	36. Causality.
habitiveness.	12. Love of Approbation.	20. Constructiveness.	29. Order.	37. Comparison.
oncentrativeness.	13. Self-Esteem.	21. Ideality.	30. Calculation.	A. Union for Life.
ombativeness.	14. Firmness.	22. Imitation.	31. Locality.	B. Sublimity.
estructiveness.	15. Conscientiousness.	23. Wit.	32. Eventuality.	C. Human Nature.
ustativeness.	16. Hope.	24. Individuality.	33. Time.	D. Agreeableness.

nological head

must be the brain and nothing else: if so, the shape of the mind (i.e. the location of certain activities such as vision or hearing) is identical with the shape of the brain: the shape of the brain is in turn determined by the shape of the skull.

The study of phrenology was originated by F. J. Gall, and was based on the observation of lunatics in asylums. The brains of different animals were also adduced in evidence. That part of phrenology which dealt with the location of motor or other simple activities has never been discredited, and we still attribute different functions to different groups of nerve cells within the brain. Phrenology went one stage further than this, because it concerned itself with the way in which emotions or complex characteristics such as a propensity to build things ('the organ of constructiveness') or to criminality ('low forehead') were displayed on the surface of the skull. Moral tendencies were also predetermined, but the existence of an area devoted to 'benevolence' was especially striking. This seemed to speak out in sharp opposition to the orthodox Christian view that human beings exhibited original sin.

Nevertheless it was a deterministic doctrine, a view neatly summed up in the following sentences, spoken by a character called Mr Cranium in Thomas Love Peacock's *Headlong Hall* (1815):

> every man's actions are determined by his peculiar views, and those views are determined by the organisation of his skull. A man in whom the organ of benevolence is not developed, cannot be benevolent: he, in whom it is so, cannot be otherwise.

In the early nineteenth century phrenology became a national movement; Spurzheim, Gall's disciple, made several lecture tours of this country, and visited the Midlands in 1830. The study of phrenology was widely taken up in the new Mechanics' Institutes, and contributed to the increasing secularisation of the beliefs of the working class. Its appeal to those who had abandoned Christianity—and here we must place Charles Bray and his new disciple Mary Ann Evans—is the key to its popularity at this time. It gave quite a different explanation of the relation of mind and body, which was totally materialistic, and its account of moral behaviour was refreshingly different from the Evangelicals'. In its day it seemed a liberating and progressive teaching, and contributed to a more humane treatment of lunatics and criminals, for example.

Its influence is everywhere apparent in the early nineteenth century, particularly on those who were intent on pushing forward the boundaries of human knowledge: Herbert Spencer, the founder of sociology (see p. 53), Robert Chambers, the author of *Vestiges of Creation*, and the biologist A. R. Wallace were all convinced phrenologists in the 1830s and 40s. Charles Bray's own conversion to the new science was brought about by a study of the works of George Combe, a now forgotten propagandist. In 1828 he had published *The Constitution of Man*, which became a best-seller: it tempered the exposition of phrenological determinism with a belief in the adaptive powers of the mind and a faith in human progress.

For Bray the discovery of Combe's liberal interpretation of phrenology had helped to clarify his thoughts after he had abandoned religious belief. As G. S. Haight dryly observes:

> To him the mind seemed subject to the same invariable rules as matter; one had only to discover the rules and act on them to be happy.... He had a plaster cast made of his head in order to examine the 'skull of the man whose character I knew best', and bought more than a hundred other casts with which to study 'the Natural Laws of the Mind'.
>
> Haight, p. 37

It is hardly a surprise to learn that Mary Ann was taken by Bray to have a cast made of her head at Deville's shop in the Strand. His description and interpretations of the result are often quoted:

> Miss Evans's head is a very large one, $22\frac{1}{4}$ inches round; George Combe, on first seeing the cast, took it for a man's ....
>
> In her brain-development the Intellect greatly predominates; it is very large, more in length than its peripheral surface. In the Feelings, the Animal and Moral regions are about equal; the moral being quite sufficient to keep the animal in order and in due subservience, but would not be spontaneously active. The social feelings were very active, particularly the adhesiveness. She was of a most affectionate disposition, always requiring some one to lean upon, preferring what has hitherto been considered the stronger sex, to the other and more impressible. She was not fitted to stand alone.
>
> Haight, p. 51

Such an acute diagnosis, however much it might be open to question as a purely phrenological case-study, remembering that Bray knew her well by this time, is nevertheless remarkable, and compares quite well with some of the psychological analyses of George Eliot which are to be found in modern biographies.

Mary Ann became a friend of Combe, after meeting him at the Brays, and continued to correspond with him for many years; he was later a supporter and a contributor when she was editing the *Westminster Review*. After she met G. H. Lewes, who was in his own way a 'real' scientist, she took the subject of phrenology less seriously. But it is worth considering how much she learnt from the serious attention which phrenology paid to mental and moral behaviour in her analysis of character in her own fiction.

On many occasions she relates personal characteristics to phrenological appearance in a way which seems strange to us; so of course does Charlotte Brontë, and the fact that both these were in their day very widely read indicates that there was nothing particularly obscure in such references. Sometimes the joke is still legible, as in the throwaway aside:

> a portrait of George the Fourth in all the majesty of his depressed cranium and voluminous neck-cloth.
> *The Mill on the Floss*, Bk 4, Ch. 3, p. 374

In *Felix Holt* the hero discusses rival views of his own character, one of which is phrenological (p. 148) and is not taken seriously. Other instances are more worth studying, however, because they seem to indicate that, even if the bumps on the skull are not referred to, the deeper teachings of phrenology remained with her as *true* perceptions of human behaviour.

On many occasions George Eliot expresses a deterministic view of character, that is, that moral behaviour is governed by laws which will inevitably lead to certain consequences. This is perhaps best exemplified in the counsel which Mr Irwine gives to Arthur in Chapter 16 of *Adam Bede*:

> A man can never do anything at variance with his own nature. He carries within him the germ of his most exceptional action ...
> p. 217

which leads to the effect on others:

> Consequences are unpitying. Our deeds carry their terrible consequences ... consequences that are hardly ever confined to ourselves.
> ibid.

For some characters in her fiction opportunities for amelioration *may* present themselves—one thinks of Janet and her 'repentance', Hetty's final conversion, and Fred Vincy's plodding climb out of debt and dishonour—but others behave like clocks that have been wound up. This may be said of even some of her greatest creations, Maggie who is carried along by the tide, and Tito in *Romola* who will never accept his responsibilities to others. For these and many others there is a chain of causality which will lead to a predetermined future. Although this may seem a very simplified account of the moral teaching which is given the full backing of George Eliot's mature deliberations on human nature, the origin of that teaching is to be sought in the phrenological textbooks which she read in her youth.

The right books at the right time

> 'If Mr Casaubon read German he would save himself a great deal of trouble.'
> 'I do not understand you,' said Dorothea, startled and anxious.
> 'I merely mean,' said Will, in an offhand way, 'that the Germans have taken the lead . . . .'
>
> *Middlemarch*, Ch. 21, p. 240

The German school of Higher Criticism has already been referred to in the discussion of Charles Hennell's book (p. 24); the Germans were far ahead of their English contemporaries in exploring new ways of reading the Bible. For many centuries scholars had confined themselves to the examination of different manuscripts and to establishing the best text from the variant readings; the Germans gave their attention to the text as a whole, and began to ask questions which were those of literary criticism. With regard to the Gospels, for example, it was necessary to establish the dates of their composition, and to consider the intentions of their authors; maybe our problems with these texts stemmed from the fact that the writers of the first century *thought* differently from ourselves. These studies diverted attention from puzzles about the literal meaning of the text, and from a fundamentalist interpretation of it.

In the previous generation of British intellectuals, only Samuel Taylor Coleridge had been aware of German scholarship; now Mary Ann Evans was to be responsible for the translation of two of the most important German works for the benefit of her English contemporaries. The first project occupied her from 1844 to 1846. Originally the translation of *Das Leben Jesu* by David Friedrich Strauss had been undertaken by Rufa Brabant, but she had not been able to get very far into the book. Mary Ann began her stint in the middle of a paragraph; as she progressed she compared notes with Sara Hennell. One can only admire the strength of character which drove her through such a long book: there are 1,500 pages in the original German. She must have worked extremely rapidly and had time for very little else—'When I can work fast I am never weary, nor do I regret either that the work has been begun, or that I have undertaken it.' (*Letters*, I 176.) In this mood she progressed at the rate of six pages a day. But on other occasions her tiredness was visible to her friends; Mrs Bray reported that Mary Ann

> was Strauss-sick—it made her ill dissecting the beautiful story of the crucifixion, and only the sight of her Christ-image and picture made her endure it.
>
> *Letters*, I 206

Strauss's book built upon the discoveries of the German school of Higher Criticism in both a negative and a positive way. He believed that *myth*, in the larger meaning of the word as a poetic construction which contains symbolic representations of eternal truths, was the appropriate medium for the expression of religious experience. The Gospels should be carefully scrutinised so that myth could be distinguished from history. A good many of the more difficult concepts of Christian belief, such as the Resurrection, would then be found to fall into the category of myth rather than history. Having lost one kind of faith, it might still be possible for a Christian to live honourably in the light of this new knowledge, and Strauss counsels the pastor, for example, to stay at his post notwithstanding. It is difficult to see how this would really be any solution, as anybody who had gone the whole way with Strauss's arguments would not be able to justify the retention of even a nominal Christian belief.

When, at long last, the work of translation was brought to an end, Mary Ann was able to resume her normal life; but at least she had been, as it were, 'blooded' as an author, and was able to understand how a long book could be carried through. *The Life of Jesus Critically Examined by Dr. David Strauss* was published on 15 June 1846. Though the translator's name was not indicated, the fact that the book was published by Chapman Bros of 121 Newgate Street, London, may be noted as an important pointer to the future. Mary Ann received a fee of £20 for her pains, but more important was the consideration that the book in some sense established her as an intellectual and a potential author herself.

The effect of the book was negligible, except on a few readers. The English were not attuned to this kind of speculation, and the idea that Christianity was a myth was not a doctrine likely to stir up revolution among the mass of believers. However, a poem by Arthur Hugh Clough, who was at the time a fellow of an Oxford college, and eventually 'lost his Faith' as a result of reading this book among others, may be adduced as evidence of the effect of the translation upon some members of the intellectual élite:

EPI-STRAUSS-IUM

Matthew and Mark and Luke and holy John
Evanished all and gone!
Yea, he that erst his dusky curtains quitting,
Thro' Eastern pictured panes his level beams transmitting,
With gorgeous portraits blent,

Christ *by Bertel Thorvaldsen, 1821. Mary Ann's Christ-image was a cast of this.*

> On them his glories intercepted spent,
> Southwestering now, thro' windows plainly glassed,
> On the inside face his radiance keen hath cast,
> And in the lustre lost, invisible and gone,
> Are, say you, Matthew, Mark and Luke and holy John?
> Lost, is it, lost, to be recovered never?
> However,
> The place of worship the meantime with light
> Is, if less richly, more sincerely bright,
> And in blue skies the Orb is manifest to sight.

Its effect upon Mary Ann herself is less easy to decide upon; in her case it must be said that she had already arrived at this position, with Hennell's aid, by 1842, and did not really learn anything new from the work; her second translation, which she was engaged upon in the early 1850s, was far more influential upon her later career as a novelist, and may be said to have transformed her beliefs. This was *The Essence of Christianity* by Ludwig Feuerbach.

Feuerbach may well be a familiar name to many readers because his work provoked Karl Marx into writing the *Theses on Feuerbach*; one of these contains the famous sentence

> Philosophers have hitherto attempted to understand the world: the thing to do is to change it.

It would be wrong however to assume from this that Feuerbach was unimportant or ineffective. Born in 1804, he studied under Hegel at Berlin; but he reacted against Hegel's metaphysical beliefs, which postulated the idea of pure thought as the centre of the universe. One of Feuerbach's works began with the statement: 'I am a real, a sensuous, a material being; yes, the body in its totality is my ego, my being itself.' He went on to say: 'I am a world removed from those philosophers who pluck out their eyes that they may think better'; this remark comes out transformed in a speech by Adam Bede:

> there's such a thing as being over-speritial ... you'd think a man must be doing nothing all's life but shutting's eyes and looking what's a-going on inside him.
>
> *Adam Bede*, Ch. 1, p. 53

Feuerbach made it clear that he had no time for the Absolute Mind of Hegel. If 'God' meant anything at all, 'He' was to be found in the relations between human beings.

The Essence of Christianity begins by establishing that the supernatural aspects of religion are a lie. Yet, paradoxically, Judaism and Christianity are both to be seen as progressive attempts to free Man from false supernatural beliefs, and in their initial stages must have appeared to be, as it were, kinds of Atheism. Feuerbach now calls upon his readers to embrace the next stage of mental liberation, which is to see that religious doctrines can be made sense of if they are interpreted in a new way. That is to say, statements about God are really attempts to define the highest nature of Man. Human beings have created God in their own image, their own best image. Ideas about God may be seen to be valid if the terms are reversed; Feuerbach's most famous example is 'God is Love'. Instead of this he wishes to substitute: 'Love is God himself, and apart from it there is no God.' This love is only to be understood from the love between human beings. Always the direction of Feuerbach's thinking is to reject the general and the abstract and to rely upon the concrete and the particular. This, as we shall see in the section on 'Realism', is just the way in which George Eliot thinks the writer of fiction should proceed.

Feuerbach's book is not easy reading, but Mary Ann had improved considerably as a translator since her work on Strauss. She greatly appreciated his dry and sarcastic witticisms, though she wondered whether they would be to the taste of English readers of theology. For example, in a very modern passage, he challenges the speculative philosophers, with their 'crass mystical theories', to tell us if God can have any real existence if he is not corporeal: and if he is so, to tell us 'of what sex he is'. His teaching about the sacrament of Holy Communion is similarly down to earth. He begins by ridiculing both the Catholic and Protestant ideas of bread and wine becoming flesh and blood, whether literally or spiritually. None of this is necessary. We are meant to enjoy life, and what is more enjoyable than eating and drinking, particularly—and again the modern note is heard—particularly when many people are without sufficient food. 'Hunger and thirst destroy not only the physical but also the mental and moral powers of man; they rob him of his humanity—of understanding, of consciousness. Oh if thou shouldst ever experience such want, how wouldst thou bless and praise the natural qualities of bread and wine, which restore to thee thy humanity, thy intellect!' It is the eating and drinking which constitute the religious act; furthermore, both bread and wine are 'as to their form, products of man. ... Bread and wine typify to us the truth that Man is the true God and Saviour of Man.'

George Eliot's absorption of and, in turn, her own commitment to the propagation of the ideas of Feuerbach can easily be illustrated by observing how this practical interpretation of the Communion is made the basis of Chapter 42 of *Adam Bede*. Hetty Sorrel is on trial for the murder of her baby; Adam, who had assumed that he was going to marry an innocent woman, is in a state of great distress. Although he has gone to the town in which the trial is taking place, he cannot face attending the court. Instead, he stays in his 'dull *upper room*'; in this first sentence of the chapter an allusion is made to the institution of the Communion at the Last Supper, and it is possible to read the whole chapter on two levels, both as a story about human beings in the nineteenth century, and at the same time as a restatement of aspects of Christianity in Feuerbach's terms.

Adam's state of mind at the beginning of the chapter is one of denial; he is powerless, he shrinks from any involvement in Hetty's suffering. In the second paragraph it is suggested that his own anguish may be a baptism, an 'initiation into a new state', but when he speaks aloud (p. 472) his incoherence seems to show the disintegration of his character. His former teacher, Bartle Massey, enters the room, 'grasps his hand'—literally the human touch— and tries to get Adam to eat and drink something: it so happens that what is available is the bread and wine which Mr Irwine, the priest, has brought. Adam refuses, pushing the cup away (Agony in the Garden?), but he listens carefully to Bartle's account of the trial. He is particularly moved to hear the suffering of Martin Poyser (p. 473), and Bartle urges him to action: 'you must help poor Martin; you must show courage.' This appeal is followed by Adam drinking a little wine. He is then able to listen to the account of Hetty's appearance: she is in a state of shock and cannot speak. Martin gives his evidence (p. 474) and is assisted out of the court by Mr Irwine, who is praised for his *human* rather than his priestly qualities—he is 'able to stand by a neighbour'. This account makes Adam respond by laying his hand on Bartle's arm, so relating himself to another human being. He perceives that it is his rôle to stand by Hetty as Irwine had done for his neighbour. Adam now speaks resolutely (p. 475); he has learned the need to show mercy to Hetty. At this point Bartle again asks Adam to eat 'for the love of me'; the chapter concludes with the two men sharing the bread and wine, which, in Feuerbach's words, can *restore one's humanity*; and so Adam 'stood upright again, and looked more like the Adam Bede of former days.'

I have commented upon this chapter at some length because it encapsulates so much of Feuerbach's moral teaching. In his view it was impossible to learn morality from conventional religion, which simply encourages passive egoism; instead we must *actively* sympathise with our fellow human beings. There are many examples of this teaching in George Eliot's novels, the most obvious being the slow awakening of Dorothea, and her practical involvement in Lydgate's financial troubles.

Mary Ann also adopted Feuerbach's views on morality in her personal life; the 'free union' with G. H. Lewes being a reference to the 'free bond' which Feuerbach postulated as the definition of marriage; he says that the relations between human beings are *per se* religious, and that a marriage which is based on an 'external restriction' is not a true marriage. Her decision to enter publicly upon such a free union with Lewes roughly coincided with the publication of her translation of Feuerbach in 1854. Her own name, Marian Evans, appeared on the title page.

The work was explained to the reading public by a reviewer in *The Spectator* in the following words:

> In plain English, this system is rank Atheism.

To which it may be wise to oppose the conclusion to Feuerbach's introduction to his book:

> what today is atheism, tomorrow will be religion.

Feuerbach's major thesis, that 'faith in God is therefore the faith of man in the infinitude and truth of his own nature.... The beginning, middle and end of religion is MAN,' these words are central to an understanding of the transformation of Christianity in the nineteenth century; many other influences, notably that of Comte, came together in the new Religion of Humanity. George Eliot's position as a sage or prophet of this 'church' must now be considered.

The Religion of Humanity

> The raw bacon which clumsy Molly spares from her own scanty store, that she may carry it to her neighbour's child to 'stop the fits', may be a piteously inefficacious remedy; but the generous stirring of neighbourly kindness that prompted the deed has a beneficent radiation that is not lost.
>
> *Adam Bede*, Ch. 3, p. 82

'The Religion of Humanity' was a widely used term in the nineteenth century. On the one hand it could be used to refer precisely to the new religion invented by Auguste Comte, and on the other hand to various post-Christian attempts to salvage the ethical precepts of the old religion while abandoning entirely its supernatural basis. It comes to mean, in fact, something more like a climate of opinion than an organised sect.

Auguste Comte was famous for two main ideas. The first was the new philosophy of Positivism. Since the only knowledge which could be verified was that obtained by scientific observation and experiment, there was no longer any point in metaphysical speculation. Having abandoned the notion of 'God' and all that that entailed, we should confine ourselves to the admittedly limited pursuit of what could be known from science. This point of view was the culmination of a way of thinking about the world which had steadily gained ground since the eighteenth century. After the 1840s it was widely accepted among the intellectual classes, and had many adherents in England.

Comte, however, was not content to leave things at that. It was still necessary to construct something in the place of what had been destroyed. In this he shows himself to be a nineteenth-century rather than an eighteenth-century thinker. He therefore proposed his second idea, a new religion, which would adhere to the tenets of Positivism, and would be called 'the Religion of Humanity'. It was to be modelled on the Catholic Church, and would contain within it orders and officials. Comte himself would fulfil the rôle of the first High Priest.

With the first of these ideas George Eliot came to agree entirely. Though she would have known about Comte earlier, his real influence on her is to be dated from the year 1853. At this time a translation of Comte's *Positive Philosophy* was published; it was the work of Harriet Martineau. It was also at this time that she came under the influence of G. H. Lewes, who was an ardent Comtean. From that 'faith' she never wavered until her last years, and it is not clear how much she really modified her opinions even then. For many years she subscribed to the London Comte Fund and was for a time connected with its 'church'; but in general she was impatient with the Comtists who tried to make her take a more active part in its organisation.

George Eliot's own religion of humanity is far more broadly based. It brings together the theological ideas of Feuerbach, the scientific approach to morality which she had learned from the phrenologists and from Comte, and a certain sternness which goes back perhaps to her Evangelical upbringing. Religion is an opium which we must learn to do without, we must make the best of this life because there is no other—these are the hard things which a grown-up person must now recognise. But in her case all is blended with a sympathy for individual cases, a wish to retain the best of what Christianity had to offer, and a warmth of feeling which she had perhaps originally absorbed from the poetry of Wordsworth.

George Eliot was therefore able to reach out to a wider audience than if she had been a strict Comtist. She was respected for her teachings, and the novels can be seen—to a certain extent—as parables in which the new attitudes to human experience are focused and defined. The novels, therefore, cannot be considered simply as enjoyable fictions; they are case-studies on which we can base a new morality—they present people under test, and from involving ourselves as readers in their problems we can learn to live more generously ourselves.

Sorting out the new 'religion' from the text of the novels is not easy. Of course there are times when the author's voice addresses us directly, and some points are made in a manner which may seem too obvious. But instead of dealing with the mid-nineteenth-century 'present', her novels are frequently set in a time *before* the new ideas had arrived in England, and we are presented with clergymen, for example, whose faith is *never in doubt,* and a society which accepts traditional Christian values. Only a very superficial reader would assume that the author agrees with these values herself—most early *Christian* reviewers had no doubt that she was a Comtist—but we have to learn to set against the surface appearance of the story the fact that the author adheres to a very different ideology. Otherwise we shall miss countless ironies and undercutting remarks, and, on the other hand, perhaps fail to appreciate the extent of the author's generosity.

For, after all, looking back across the gulf of experience which separates her from the characters in her stories, she could have despised her Christian heroes and heroines, and laughed at their pitiful ignorance of the new faith. Such is the usual behaviour of converts. Instead she looks for points in their lives where they unconsciously anticipated and practised the new religion of humanity, like Adam Bede in the chapter already discussed or like 'clumsy Molly' in the epigraph to this section. In Wordsworthian terms, she calls attention to their

> little nameless unremembered acts
> Of kindness and of love.

Though her longer novels have so many elements in them that a simple account of them as parable would be too reductive, an exception can be made for the case of *Silas Marner*. At first Silas is unable to relate to the community of Raveloe; his conversion is brought about through the unwitting agency of a child, who seems at first to be a supernatural apparition or a sending from another world. All is explained, however, in due course. But the result of his conversion is that he returns to society and eventually begins to attend the local church. This again is also carefully emptied of religious significance; the church is simply the appropriate *social* nexus at the time in which the story is set. The whole story of Silas is explicable in human terms; it is by human beings that he is saved and restored to a fully human life. Yet this account is too like a diagram; there remains a mystery about *Silas Marner* which allows the reader, of whatever religious persuasion, to accept the story as having unspoken dimensions.

In this way, an unsympathetic critic might observe, she was able to have her cake and eat it; she was able to obtain wide popular acclaim with a book like *Adam Bede*, which shows so much sympathy for Christianity in the character of Dinah Morris, and at the same time, by her preaching of the religion of humanity, to seem the spokesman of the new intellectual movement, and to satisfy her Positivist friends. A more constructive account would surely show that George Eliot is trying to save as much as she can of the truth in the older religion, though writing from the point of view of the new ideology. Though the breakdown of the old Christian certainties had led to the general religious crisis, and produced in so many individuals symptoms of anxiety and despair, George Eliot was able to rise above a merely personal response to the new situation. Through her teaching she was able to build bridges, for herself and others, which connected the old religion with the new.

3 Choosing

Alone in Geneva

> O the bliss of having a very high attic in a romantic continental town, such as Geneva—far away from morning callers, dinners, and decencies; and then to pause for a year and think de omnibus et quibusdam aliis, and then to return to life, and work for poor stricken humanity and never think of self again.
>
> *Letters*, I 261

This extract from a letter of 1848 outlines a private dream. When Mary Ann's father died she was at last free to choose a new way of life. In this chapter we examine the choices open to her in the early 1850s, and though three of them are connected with male companionship, this should not cause us to bewail her lack of self-sufficiency. Life for a woman on her own was not easy in the middle of the nineteenth century, and she had been conditioned to expect marriage. At first, though, she tried the single life and the development of her own personality.

On 11 June 1849, five days after her father's funeral, Mary Ann set out with the Brays on a continental tour; at the conclusion of this venture they left her at Geneva. She remained there from 25 July until March of the following year. In part this can simply be regarded as an extension of her holiday; she needed to recover from the strain of nursing her father. She was able to support herself by drawing £100 from her legacy. At first she stayed in a pension by the lake, and then moved into lodgings with a family in the town; it happened that her new host was a painter, François D'Albert Durade. He was married and forty-five years old:

> I love him already as if he were father and brother both ... he is not more that 4 feet high with a deformed spine—the result of an accident in his boyhood—but on this little body is placed a finely formed head, full in every direction.
>
> *Letters*, I 316–7

He asked for permission to paint her portrait. At the end of her stay he escorted her back to England, and she visited him in later years; he also translated many of her novels into French. It is also possible that he is in some sense the model for Philip Wakem.

The period in Geneva is not referred to in her fiction, except in the story 'The Lifted Veil'; a number of minor points indicate however that this short excursion abroad was important in changing her direction in life. She had her hair done in a new way—in the portrait her curls have been 'abolished'—and she began to keep a journal. She now signed herself 'Marian', perhaps on the analogy of the French form 'Marianne.' By living out the romantic dream she had got through a good deal of postponed 'growing up'.

John Chapman and the Westminster Review

You know she was very fond of me.

John Chapman in old age

On her return from Geneva, Mary Ann paid family visits and then decided to stay with the Brays for a while; but she was already thinking of living in London, and took the opportunity of staying at John Chapman's house in London in November 1850. This came about because Chapman had asked her to review a book by William Mackay which had been published earlier that year. It was called *The Progress of the Intellect, as exemplified in the Religious Development of the Greeks and the Hebrews*; Mackay was one of the few followers of Strauss writing in England at the time, and Mary Ann was almost the only person qualified to review it with understanding. The book contains much discussion of ancient myths, and Mackay is praised for 'the introduction of a truly philosophic spirit into the study of mythology—an introduction for which we are chiefly indebted to the Germans ...' Mackay was evidently better equipped than poor Casaubon, and yet it is interesting to see Mary Ann herself regarded as an expert in the same field as that unfortunate scholar.

Chapman's boarding-house in the Strand was famous as a kind of literary hotel; Emerson, for example, had stayed there in 1848. Having enjoyed her short visit, it was quite natural that Mary Ann should decide to return after Christmas, and to make the house her base while she tried to pursue her career as a writer; but it is also clear that, though she had met Chapman on one or two previous occasions and had heard something of his reputation, she had no idea of the kind of establishment she was moving into.

George Eliot by François D'Albert Durade, 1850

Chapman's house had a public and a private function. Since he was always on the verge of falling into debt, it was necessary to have a house large enough to accommodate boarders, who could be made to pay between 45 and 50 shillings a week; in addition it served as a literary club for Chapman's authors and business connections, who were invited there on Friday nights. On a private level it provided a home for his wife, Susanna, two of his children, and a succession of mistresses who were disposed in suitable rooms about the house. Exactly how much Susanna knew of these affairs is open to question; in 1850 the reigning beauty was Miss Elisabeth Tilley, who was described in the 1851 Census as a 'Visitor, aged 30'. Chapman kept a detailed journal of his private life, but the pages for the early months of 1851 have been mutilated so that it is not entirely clear what happened. We learn that on 8 January 'Miss Evans arrived at Euston Square at 3 P.M. where I met her, her manner was friendly but formal and studied.' By the middle of February it is clear that Elisabeth had become increasingly worried about Chapman's relationship with Miss Evans and had ganged up with Susanna against him. For example, we read on 18 February that

> I presume with a view of arriving at a more friendly understanding S. & E. had a long talk this morning which resulted in their comparing notes on the subject of my intimacy with Miss Evans, and their arrival at the conclusion that we are completely in love with each other.—E. being intensely jealous herself said all she could to cause S. to look from the same point of view, which a little incident (her finding me with my hand in M's) had quite prepared her for. E. betrayed my trust and her own promise. S. said to me that if ever I went to M's room again she will write to Mr Bray, and say that she dislikes her.

Finally, after further quarrels, we read that on 24 March

> M. departed today, I accompanied her to the railway. She was very sad, and hence made me feel so.—She pressed me for some intimation of the state of my feelings,—I told her that I felt great affection for her, but that I loved E. and S. also, though each in a different way . . . .

It is difficult to comment on a situation which verges on the ludicrous. That John Chapman was attractive to women is clear—he was known as 'Byron' in Nottingham. For Mary Ann he also represented the source of her hoped-for commissions as a 'writer'—though none were forthcoming on this occasion—and she returned to Coventry in some distress. But she was not one to give up easily; a complicated correspondence ensued, and because her letters were circulated round the household at 142 Strand she even resorted to the device of enclosing little private notes for John in the middle of business letters to Chapman.

Then, in the middle of 1851, Chapman had an amazing stroke of good fortune; one of his well-wishers enabled him to purchase the *Westminster Review* outright. He needed an editor; though he would retain the title in public, he was not capable of managing the literary side of the work. After a great deal of further negotiation he was able to note in his diary that Miss Evans had returned to London and to her old room on 29 September.

The *Westminster Review* had been founded by James Mill in 1824. From the early years of the century the great reviews—in particular the *Edinburgh*, the *Quarterly*, and *Blackwood's*—had dominated British intellectual life in a way which it is difficult to appreciate today. Books were relatively expensive, and libraries were few and far between; the reviews provided a digest of recent publications, and gave lengthy excerpts from the books which they noticed. Authors were highly paid for contributing to the reviews, but their articles were anonymous as a general rule. The *Westminster* was a liberal and secular periodical, founded to counteract the Tory or Whig bias of the other reviews; after changing hands it had returned to the editorship of a Mill, this time James's son John Stuart, from 1837 to 1840. It had then gone through an undistinguished period, though important articles continued to appear. Now Mary Ann was to write the prospectus for a new series, to commence in January 1852.

She was the editor for ten numbers; the periodical kept its political bias in favour of Reform, and had an extensive coverage of foreign affairs. These areas could be fed with commissioned articles. Mary Ann was responsible for the sub-editing, and such was the pressure of work that it is difficult to trace many original items by her during this period. However, there was a particular emphasis on contemporary literature; an enormous number of books were summarily dealt with. Any entries which may be ascribed to her may be found printed or listed in Pinney's *Essays of George Eliot*. Her contribution to the editing of the *Westminster Review* can therefore only be assessed in the most general terms, but it is worth pointing out that another periodical, the *Leader*, noted that the review had 'recovered the importance it acquired when under the editorship of John Stuart Mill'.

Herbert Spencer and the study of society

> See what a fine thing it is to pick up people who are short sighted enough to like one.
>
> *Letters*

Meanwhile Mary Ann had ceased to be involved in Chapman's love-life, though she continued to work and correspond with him on cordial terms. More and more of her free time was spent with Herbert Spencer, at this period a rising young journalist; he was the sub-editor of *The Economist*, which was produced at rooms opposite to Chapman's house in the Strand. They had much in common.

Spencer was another Midlander who was trying to make his way in London; like Mary Ann, he was to a certain extent self-taught and had embraced new ideas and liberal opinions. It was his mission to propagate a true understanding of human behaviour; he was one of the first social scientists. After a number of false starts he was taken up by Chapman, who had just published Spencer's first book; it was appropriately entitled *Social Statics, or the Conditions Essential to Human Happiness Specified, and the First of them Developed*. He was now working on *The Principles of Psychology*, which he discussed with Mary Ann; she is honoured in a footnote, but it has been suggested that she contributed more than one sentence to the book, and that in his turn Spencer influenced her later drawing of character. However, their meetings were more convivial than all this may indicate, as Spencer reviewed musical and theatrical performances for his paper and often received complimentary tickets. After a preliminary stage of pretending that they were just friends, Mary Ann was led to an avowal of love. This letter was sent from Broadstairs on 16 July 1852:

> I know this letter will make you very angry with me, but wait a little, and don't say anything to me while you are angry. I promise not to sin any more in the same way.
>
> My ill health is caused by the hopeless wretchedness which weighs upon me. I do not say this to pain you, but because it is the simple truth which you must know in order to understand why I am obliged to seek relief.
>
> I want to know if you can assure me that you will not forsake me, that you will always be with me as much as you can and share your thoughts and feelings with me. If you become attached to some one else, then I must die, but until then I could gather courage to work and make life valuable, if only I had you near me. I do not ask you to sacrifice anything—I would be very good and cheerful and never annoy you. But I find it impossible to contemplate life under any other conditions. If I had your assurance, I could trust that and live upon it. I have struggled— indeed I have—to renounce everything and be entirely unselfish, but I find myself utterly unequal to it. Those who have known me best have always said, that if ever I loved any one thoroughly my whole life must turn upon that feeling, and I find they said truly. You curse the destiny which has made the feeling concentrate itself on you—but if you will only have patience with me

you shall not curse it long. You will find that I can be satisfied with very little, if I am delivered from the dread of losing it.

I suppose no woman ever before wrote such a letter as this—but I am not ashamed of it, for I am conscious that in the light of reason and true refinement I am worthy of your respect and tenderness, whatever gross men or vulgar-minded women might think of me.

Letters, VIII 56–7

Spencer appears to have been unable to return such affection, and a number of more or less cruel anecdotes are related about him; he is said to have lamented her lack of beauty. Whether or not he really cared about her, he had missed his chance. By 1853 G. H. Lewes was in the ascendant, and Spencer entered upon a kind of nervous breakdown, alleviated only by taking long walks. He never married, but kept George Eliot's photograph by him until his death.

Although Spencer failed to come up to scratch, it would be unfair to treat him as merely having a slight influence upon George Eliot. He was the founding father of sociology, however unrecognisable his work might appear to a modern sociologist; society is to be scientifically observed, and it is worth noting that *Middlemarch* is subtitled 'A study of Provincial Life'. In *Social Statics* he expressed the view that woman was an independent being and the equal of man, a view that George Eliot's life and novels substantiate. In later life he claimed that he was the first to advise her to write novels. Spencer is not an easy person to warm to; like Ladislaw, he was one of the 'new people' that the nineteenth century gave birth to, and I suspect that that young journalist may share some of *his* more maddening characteristics.

Love and Mr Lewes

in the seventies and eighties of the last century, apparently, to discard marital obligations was commonly called 'living à la George Eliot.'

Anne Fremantle, *George Eliot* (1933)

At first sight George Henry Lewes would not appear to have been attractive, either in appearance or in character. His friends called him 'Ape', and children were alleged to run away from him in horror. On the whole, though, the negative judgements are made by men; for example, George Meredith described him as a 'mercurial little showman.' Women found him more interesting; Charlotte Brontë met him in 1850, and reported that

the aspect of Lewes's face almost moved me to tears; it is so wonderfully like Emily, her eyes, her features, the very nose, the

somewhat prominent mouth, the forehead, even, at moments, the expression; whatever Lewes does or says, I believe I cannot hate him.

Even Eliza Lynn Linton, who disliked him intensely, conceded that 'wherever he went there was always a patch of intellectual sunshine in the room.' A little vitality seems to have gone a long way in Victorian society, and uninhibited behaviour, such as Lewes seems to have been capable of, was no doubt a welcome relief.

Lewes was two years older than Mary Ann; he had left school in 1833, and since then had lived by his wits. His career had so far combined the rôles of lecturer, actor, journalist and historian of philosophy; he also wrote plays under the name of Slingsby Lawrence, and had become a frequent contributor to the *Westminster Review*. From the fringes of the literary world he had moved towards its centre, and as he grew older his books became better rather than worse. A convinced Positivist, he tried to train himself to observe phenomena like a scientist, and there is nothing like 'keeping one's eye on the object' as a recipe for success in literature. His versatility was amazing, and his output astonishing.

Mary Ann first met him on 6 October 1851, but she only got to know him some time later. She began to take him seriously from the autumn of 1852, after the charms of Herbert Spencer had ceased to amuse. In September 1853 she moved out of Chapman's 'literary hotel', presumably so that she and Lewes could begin to live together inconspicuously, though the evidence for this is hearsay only. The die was finally cast when she left for Germany with him on 20 July 1854, and began to describe herself as his 'wife'.

This, however, she was not, nor ever could be. Lewes had married Agnes Jervis in 1841. As a disciple of the poet Shelley, he did not believe in the restrictions of the conventional code, and after the years of first love had waned he was content to share his wife with Thornton Hunt, while he pursued his own path. Traditional moralists have been hard on Lewes, seeing him as a lustful satyr who used Shelley's ideas as a cover for his 'crimes', but it seems more reasonable to see him as a genuine admirer of Shelley who had experimented with new forms of communal living. Such things were very much in the air in the 1840s, and received some intellectual justification from the writings of Comte, who had announced that the old social order was about to collapse. Meanwhile, the old laws of the land still held sway; when, in 1850, Agnes bore her first child to Thornton Hunt, Lewes had been reluctant to declare the child illegitimate and had acknowledged it as his own; this meant that he forfeited the right to sue his wife for adultery, and so could

G. H Lewes from a watercolour by Anne Gliddon c. 1840

not divorce her. It would be fair to say, though, that his marriage had broken down completely by the time he met Mary Ann though he continued to support Agnes and her children for the rest of his life.

Even if legal grounds for divorce had been available, it was an expensive process. Lewes lived from hand to mouth, and Mary Ann did not present any financial attractions at this time. When they 'eloped' to Germany their only income was from occasional articles which were accepted by English magazines. After a chance meeting with Strauss at Cologne, they proceeded to Weimar; the intention was to interview the friends and relatives of the poet Goethe, whose biography Lewes was engaged in writing. Mary Ann was able to help Lewes with the German language; when it was published, the book became a standard work.

In March 1855 they returned to England; they lived in various lodgings as Mr and Mrs Lewes; their frequent changes of address may well have been prompted by attempts to avoid being 'found out', and friends were upbraided for writing to 'Marian Evans'. Whatever Feuerbach may have meant by the 'free bond of marriage', the forbidden relationship led Mary Ann into deceit, equivocation and even downright lying. On 8 May 1856 a happier time began; they went to Ilfracombe and Tenby to enable G. H. Lewes to work on his *Seaside Studies*; in spite of the title this was to be a popular yet thorough and authoritative scientific work. It was at this time that Lewes encouraged Mary Ann to try her hand at fiction.

From this point onwards Lewes is best seen as George Eliot's agent. The relationship was transformed. George Eliot became the breadwinner—in fact her books soon brought them riches. Lewes, on the other hand, dealt with publishers and editors, and carefully censored any 'upsetting' reviews of her work. The fact that her books are mainly concerned with social relationships in her Midlands past may be summarily dealt with at this point, whatever else we may need to add later—in the early years with Lewes she had NO social relationships in the present. Lewes could still go anywhere he liked and be accepted into any house he chose to visit; *she* on the other hand could not be invited out to dinner or to any gathering where 'proper' wives were present; in the social code of the time she was a mistress, a kept woman. Though in later years her position as a 'famous writer' brought some amelioration, she was still impossible to 'place' socially because of her relationship with Lewes. As Lord Acton said after her death:

> Ostensibly in accepting Lewes she was resigning a small group of friends, and an obscure position in literature. What she really sacrificed was liberty of speech, the foremost rank among the women of her time, and a tomb in Westminster Abbey.

4 Towards fiction

Realism

> The mine of real life
> Dig for us; and present us, in the shape
> Of virgin ore, that gold which we, by pains
> Fruitless as those of aery alchemists,
> Seek from the torturing crucible. There lies
> Around us a domain where you have long
> Watched both the outward course and inner heart:
> Give us, for our abstractions, solid facts;
> For our disputes, plain pictures.
>
> Wordsworth, *The Excursion*, V. 630–8

Because 'realism' has been so much a matter for literary debate in recent years, it may be said that the term has become quite meaningless. I propose therefore to restrict the discussion to the vogue which the word enjoyed in the 1850s, largely as the result of George Eliot's own employment of it as a slogan in what might be described as her 'propaganda'.

There is evidence that the same worries which led her to adopt the doctrine of Realism in the 1850s were present to her from an early age. In a letter to Maria Lewis of 16 March 1839 she explains that

> When a person has exhausted the wonders of truth, there is no other resort than fiction.

This could be described as a rather pompous remark by a fanatical nineteen-year-old Evangelical in correspondence with her mentor; the general context is a discussion of novels, and whether it is right to read them at all. She considers that an educated person should be content with history, although she allows that standard authors such as Scott and Cervantes must be known. Otherwise she sees no use for a 'phantom conjured up by fancy', and advertises the fact that she is undertaking such worthwhile reading as the *Life of Wilberforce*.

However, if we take the remark totally out of context and apply it to the *writing* of novels, it demonstrates exactly the attitudes which George Eliot adopted as a reviewer of contemporary literature in the 1850s. Writers should keep their eyes on what is set before them, instead of embroidering fancies or 'fictions' which have no basis in reality. In an article written in 1856, just before she began work on 'Amos Barton', she attacked 'Silly Novels by Lady Novelists':

> the most mischieveous form of feminine silliness is the literary form.

Why? Because women tend to write 'froth': it is interesting that this is a word which she had used in the letter of 1839 already quoted. The point is made again and again in a series of pleasant jokes; the ladies will not undertake what George Eliot regards as the necessary work of observation. They cannot keep their eyes on the real world:

> Lady novelists, it appears, can see something else besides matter; they are not limited to phenomena, but can relieve their eyesight by occasional glimpses of the *noumenon*.

At thirty-six George Eliot is more confident than she had been at nineteen, but she is after the same quarry; most of what goes under the name of 'fiction' is, as the word implies, invented and untrue. It is therefore sheer rubbish, and she is determined to have none of it. Later, in a letter to Blackwood of 30 March 1861, she will speak of 'the high responsibilities of literature that undertakes to represent life'.

In order to make clear her positive requirements from a writer of novels, she employs a term that had been used for some time in the criticism of art. 'Réalisme' had been used by the French to describe the work of Rembrandt, and the fact that he was a Dutch painter is to be noted. In 1856 the word had sufficient vogue in France to be used as the title of a new journal, and it is in the same year that George Eliot uses the word herself for the first time. Because it was unfamilar to her readers it is italicised and explained; in a review of Volume III of Ruskin's *Modern Painters* she announces that

> The truth of infinite value that he teaches is *realism*—the doctrine that all truth and beauty are to be attained by a humble and faithful study of nature, and not by substituting vague forms, bred by imagination on the mists of feeling, in place of definite,

Christ in the house of his parents *by John Everett Millais, 1850*

substantial reality. The thorough acceptance of this doctrine would remould our life....

A parallel movement in English art in the 1850s was Pre-Raphaelitism. Ruskin was the champion of the painters of this school, and had even found something to admire in Millais's *Christ in the house of his parents*, which Dickens and others had laughed to scorn. George Eliot did not, however, link herself to this school, though we shall see that she praised Holman Hunt's painting *The Hireling Shepherd* for the reality of its landscape (p. 83). Instead, probably because of her familiarity with French usage, she went back through Rembrandt to 'Dutch painting' in order to find a model for the novelist's art. The most well-known exposition of this analogy is in Chapter 17 of *Adam Bede*:

> It is for this rare, precious quality of truthfulness that I delight in many Dutch paintings, which lofty-minded people despise. I find a source of delicious sympathy in these faithful pictures of a monotonous homely existence, which has been the fate of so many more among my fellow-mortals than a life of pomp or of absolute indigence, of tragic suffering or of world-stirring actions. I turn without shrinking from cloud-borne angels, from prophets, sibyls, and heroic warriors, to an old woman bending over her flower-pot, or eating her solitary dinner, while the noonday light, softened perhaps by a screen of leaves, falls on her mob-cap, and just touches the rim of her spinning-wheel, and her stone jug, and all those cheap common things which are the precious necessaries of life to her;—or I turn to that village wedding, kept between four brown walls, where an awkward bridegroom opens the dance with a high-shouldered, broad-faced bride, while elderly and middle-aged friends look on, with very irregular noses and lips, and probably with quart pots in their hands, but with an expression of unmistakable contentment and good-will. 'Foh!' says my idealistic friend, 'what vulgar details! What good is there in taking all these pains to give an exact likeness of old women and clowns? What a low phase of life! — what clumsy, ugly people!'
>
> *Adam Bede*, p. 223

On the next page of the novel she contrasts 'the divine beauty of form' which has been the subject of so much other painting with

> that other beauty too, which lies in no secret of proportion, but in the secret of deep human sympathy. Paint us an angel, if you can, with a floating violet robe, and a face paled by the celestial light; paint us yet oftener a Madonna, turning her mild face up-

A Woman Scraping Parsnips *by Nicholas Maes, 1655*

> ward and opening her arms to welcome the divine glory; but do not impose on us any aesthetic rules which shall banish from the region of Art those old women scraping carrots with their work-worn hands, those heavy clowns taking holiday in a dingy pot-house, those rounded backs and stupid weather-beaten faces that have bent over the spade and done the rough work of the world —those homes with their tin pans, their brown pitchers, their rough curs, and their clusters of onions. In this world there are so many of these common, coarse people, who have no picturesque sentimental wretchedness! It is so needful we should remember their existence, else we may happen to leave them quite out of our religion and philosophy, and frame lofty theories which only fit a world of extremes. Therefore let Art always remind us of them....
>
> Adam Bede, p. 224

Setting aside George Eliot's constant reference to painting, how much of this paragraph reads like a paraphrase of Feuerbach—no longer do we require pictures of divine Madonnas, but of human sympathy.

I have tried to demonstrate that George Eliot's doctrine of realism is a coming together of different interests which had been with her for many years, perhaps related in origin, as I suggested in Chapter 1, to her father's attitude to work. Certainly what emerges is a logical extension of Feuerbach's Religion of Humanity, and at this stage of her career it provides a lever with which she is poised to move the earth. The problem, though, which must confront any honest reading of George Eliot's novels, always excepting *Daniel Deronda*, is that this theory should lead to novels about *contemporary reality*, instead of what might pass for historical novels about the early nineteenth century. You would have expected this burning new faith to confront the problems of the 1850s, 60s and 70s head on.

In this, like the Pre-Raphaelites, she seems to have been unable to deliver the goods; Rossetti turned out canvas after canvas set in the romantic medieval past, but could never finish *Found*, which is almost his only important non-medieval work. Another Pre-Raphaelite, William Morris, comments acidly about one aspect of realism in *News from Nowhere*:

> It is true that in the nineteenth century, when there was so little art and so much talk about it, there was a theory that art and imaginative literature ought to deal with contemporary life; but they never did so....

The reason, according to Morris's speaker, is that

> it is the child-like part of us that produces works of imagination.

Simple though this may sound, it leads us into a deeper examination of George Eliot's case.

Wordsworth and the power of memory

> at present my mind works with the most freedom and the keenest sense of poetry in my remotest past, and there are many strata to be worked through before I can begin to use *artistically* any material I may gather in the present.
>
> Letter to Barbara Bodichon, 11 August 1859

George Eliot's inability to write directly about the present can be accounted for in several ways. Some are more or less obvious and need not detain us for long. In any age it has never been easy to write convincingly about contemporary life—I mean a deep analysis of social behaviour, rather than a journalistic account of fashionable trends. How many of us could put together a comprehensive novel which showed that we really understood the implications of living in the Computer Age? Secondly, it has always been necessary to step back a little from one's subject in order to see it whole. Thirdly, the events of early life strike a more vivid impression into the mind than those of mature years, and the psychological phenomenon of very old people being able to recall their childhood in detail, having forgotten the intervening period, is well known.

George Eliot was not an old person, however, and I don't think that any of the above reasons will do in her case. There seems to have been something special about the nineteenth century, in that it inspired its more sensitive children not just to transcend but to escape from the present. In the first place, most writers, after an initial flush of enthusiasm, united to condemn the industrial towns as peculiarly sordid, and artists by and large avoided them, preferring to imagine themselves living at the time of Dante. By their very name and their principal choice of subject-matter the Pre-Raphaelite painters typified this mental attitude, which was at variance with the realistic surface of their work; architects, too, attempted to revive the Gothic style, and even George Eliot, in spite of the implications of her realism, felt that a novel about medieval Florence (*Romola*) was what the age demanded. Secondly, the railways seem to have disoriented people; their development was unplanned, and their rapidity gave rise to a feeling that the pace of life had accelerated and that the 'Old England' had gone for good. The introduction to *Felix Holt*, which depicts the English countryside as seen from the box of a horse-drawn coach, could be taken as an appeal to the reader to indulge himself in sentimental contemplation of the vanished past.

The pressures of living in the new cities of the nineteenth century were a common theme of poetry. Matthew Arnold, for example, speaks of 'this strange disease of modern life', and suggested that one source of healing was to be found in the poetry of William Wordsworth. Here could be discovered 'the freshness of the early world.' Intellectuals generally were thought to suffer as a result of over-cerebral mental activies; John Stuart Mill states in his *Autobiography* that

> the habit of analysis has a tendency to wear away the feelings . . .

In this case this had led to deeper and deeper depression, from which he had been rescued by reading Wordsworth.

This is not the place for a full exposition of Wordsworth's teaching. In well-known poems, such as the 'Lines' usually called 'Tintern Abbey', he had already diagnosed the disease, and suggested a cure. For those condemned to live in the modern city, remembrances of the past, particularly of natural objects, could provide 'tranquil restoration'; his own visit to Tintern Abbey would generate 'life and food / For future years.' This was written as early as 1798; a later poem, the 'Ode' on 'Intimations of Immortality from Recollections of Early Childhood', insists on the power of our earliest memories, and suggests that by keeping them alive within us we retain a link back to our true origins; these are assumed, in the poem, to be divine—

> trailing clouds of glory do we come
> From God, who is our home . . . .

but Wordsworth's constant use of the words 'Man' and 'human', culminating in

> Thanks to the human heart by which we live,

keep the poem firmly rooted in this world. *The Prelude* explained the doctrine at length; only by keeping our memories of childhood alive can our emotional life remain healthy. Wordsworth narrates his own case to prove this, and shows how he had re-integrated his personality after a kind of breakdown; this in turn had led to a release of creative power.

Wordsworth's influence on George Eliot is now to be considered. We have already seen how her early reading of the poet was part of her intellectual awakening. She re-read him after translating Strauss—a possible example of 'over-cerebral activity'—and he seems to have been constantly in her mind during the composition of her early novels. *Adam Bede* and *Silas Marner* both have epigraphs from Wordsworth's poems; furthermore, in *Adam Bede* she mentions the *Lyrical Ballads*, where Wordsworth had been her forerunner in exploring the presence of the deeper emotions in 'low and rustic life'. *Silas Marner*, it might be said, is a Lyrical Ballad in prose; Silas resembles some of the knottier Wordsworthian characters, and it is significant that he finds restoration in middle life through the agency of a child. In fact, George Eliot said that Wordsworth would have been the ideal reader (*Letters*, III 382).

It seems to me that George Eliot underwent a similar experience to Silas and Wordsworth himself; living in the great city, and having by this time largely broken with her family, she had needed to re-establish continuity with her own childhood and her rural past. To do this, again like Wordsworth, she relied on the power of memory rather than on immediate experience:

> the secret of our emotions never lies in the bare object but in its subtle relations to our own past.
>
> *Adam Bede*, Ch. 18, p. 245

Later she sees herself as a teacher of the Wordsworthian doctrine, and we can find many examples in *The Mill on the Floss*. On page 94 she meditates upon Tom and Maggie's early years, and then opens the discussion towards her readers:

> These familiar flowers, these well-remembered bird-notes.... such things as these are the mother tongue of our imagination, the language that is laden with all the subtle inextricable associations the fleeting hours of our childhood left behind them. Our delight in the sunshine on the deep bladed grass today, might be no more than the faint perception of wearied souls, if it were not for the sunshine and the grass in the far-off years, which still live in us and transform our perceptions into love.

This passage, like that about the elderberry bush on page 222, teach us joy in common things, and must have also served to reassure readers disturbed by the change and bustle of the mid-century that it was possible to find a route back that was also, paradoxically, a way forwards. Having first healed herself, she was able to extend sympathy to others; the fact that this transforming process was accompanied by a literal change of name does not seem particularly remarkable.

Becoming George Eliot

> the female pen is capable of writing a very bad novel, when wilful women set their wits that way
>
> George Eliot in a review of 1854

When G. H. Lewes sent the publisher John Blackwood the manuscript of 'Amos Barton' on 6 November 1856, he enclosed a letter explaining that it had been written by a 'friend who desired my good offices,' and who was referred to in the same letter as 'he'. This soon developed (on 15 November) into 'my clerical friend', so that Blackwood replied 'I am glad to hear that your friend is as I supposed a clergyman.' Lewes felt that he had to deny this vocation, but insisted on his friend's anonymity. When 'Amos Barton' had been published in *Blackwood's* the new writer was identified as 'George Eliot', though it was made clear that this was a *nom de plume*. Many years later J. W. Cross said that he had been told that this pseudonym had been compiled in the following way: 'George' was Lewes's Christian name, and 'Eliot' was an easily pronounced word. This explanation is unconvincing, as is the suggestion that it resembles a Cockney pronunciation of Lewes's name—'George 'Enry Loos'. Since the object of the exercise was to *preserve anonymity*, there would be no point in giving a lead to those who knew about her association with Lewes in the first place. Those who were not privy to her 'marriage', that is her new reading public, would also ask why she was connected with him.

It is worth observing that it is at this time—1857—that Marian Evans wrote to her family and friends to tell them that she wished to be known as Marian Lewes. She was disconcerted by the coldness with which the news was received. By the end of the year she had revealed her identity as 'George Eliot' in confidence to Herbert Spencer; then came unforeseen difficulties, as the 'originals' of the characters in the *Scenes of Clerical Life*, or their relatives, began to write in to Blackwood. There were also attempts to impersonate 'George Eliot', the most notable one being a Mr Liggins from the Isle of Man. She revealed her identity to Blackwood on 28 February 1858, but the anonymity was preserved until the publication of *Adam Bede* made it impossible to fob off her family and friends. Nevertheless, she did not abandon the pseudonym, and continued to call herself 'George Eliot' in print from this time until her death, except for the *Impressions of Theophrastus Such*, which were said to be 'edited by George Eliot' and fooled nobody.

There are a number of practical observations to be made at this point. In the first place, pseudonyms were a feature of nineteenth-century literature; some people had several, one advantage being that the 'name' of an obviously unsuccessful 'writer' could be shed like an old coat. Secondly, the name of Marian Evans had only been used on the title-page of one of her previous works, the translation of Feuerbach; her other work had been unsigned—magazine articles usually were at this time, as was the tradition in *The Times* until quite recently. Although she now insisted on calling herself 'Mrs Lewes'—in private life—this name could not have been used for reasons of propriety; *Blackwood's* would not have been prepared to explain how there had come to be two 'Mrs Leweses'. This would have lost them their 'family readership' at a stroke, and it was pointed out later, when the secret came out after the publication of *Adam Bede*, that had the marital status of the author been known the critics would have united to 'forbid' decent readers to buy such 'vicious' work.

Deeper considerations now intrude themselves. Why did she wish to be taken for a man? As we have already seen, the author of the essay 'Silly Novels by Lady Novelists' had nailed her colours to the mast: she would obviously not wish to be associated with such people. In later years she was most hurt when she was consigned to their company; after an article in a French journal had committed this solecism she was affronted:

> The most ignorant journalist in England would hardly think of calling me a rival of Miss Mulock, a writer who is read only by novel readers, pure and simple, never by people of high culture.

A number of revealing prejudices are betrayed here, and it comes as rather a shock to learn that Miss Mulock, afterwards known as Mrs Craik, was the author of *John Halifax, Gentleman*.

Also to be considered is the example of Charlotte Brontë, who had called herself 'Currer Bell', and, across the Channel, that of George Sand, whose novels George Eliot had devoured in 1846: I cannot believe that the name of 'George' has no reference to the French precursor. Years later, in *Daniel Deronda*, there is the illuminating remark:

> You may try, but you can never imagine what it is to have a man's force of genius in you, and yet to suffer the slavery of being a girl.

Whether or not she felt this, a case could be made that she did need to create a new literary personaality for herself at this time, whether to be free of the Liberal journalist in her, or to satisfy some obscurer need. After commencing as a writer of novels she wrote very few articles, apart from a short reappearance as a reviewer when G. H. Lewes took on the editorship of the *Fortnightly* in 1865. While not pretending that we have as startling a change as that from Eric Blair to 'George Orwell', where it can be argued that a remaking of the personality took place, the new name did seem to produce a stimulus and a release; she moved boldly forward into new literary territory, in spite of the pathological shyness 'as a person' which G. H. Lewes refers to.

5 Later years

Showing that old acquaintances are capable of surprising us
> All perfection in this life is accompanied by a measure of imperfection, and all our knowledge contains an element of obscurity.
>
> Thomas à Kempis

George Eliot's later years are mainly the record of her writings with holidays and the preparations for the next book filling the intervening spaces. It is a tale of ever-increasing financial success and an extremely rapid rise to fame; after the publication of *Romola*, it is true, there was an indeterminate period when she seemed to have lost her way, but this was soon succeeded by the achievement of *Middlemarch* and the vigorous experiment of *Daniel Deronda*.

As time went on, there is evidence that she began to behave in the manner expected of a famous author, and eventually turned herself into the Sibylline oracle, or so some would have us believe. Of course, common sense interjects, people do alter, and it is annoying when our friends become famous and leave us behind. But the general picture of the majestic presence is confirmed by kind friends as well as unkind purveyors of gossip. One admires John Blackwood for daring to write to her in 1874:

> If you have any lighter pieces written before the sense of what a great author should do for mankind came so strongly upon you, I should like much to look at them.

In 1863 the Leweses' financial security was such that they were able to purchase The Priory, on the North Bank of the Regent's Park Canal. The house was decorated and furnished throughout by the fashionable designer, Mr Owen Jones. The Leweses were now able to entertain, and the gatherings on Sunday afternoons at The Priory became part of the London social round. At first only a small group of intimates attended, but in the 1870s G. H. Lewes wrote that 'Lords and Ladies, poets and cabinet ministers, artists and men of science, crowd upon us.' The order of these notabilities

The Priory, North Bank, St John's Wood

tells one a good deal about the values which Lewes held, and it is important to realise that men predominate: ladies could not be invited to The Priory, but were welcome if they were prepared to take the social risk of attending.

'Mrs Lewes generally sat in an armchair at the left of the fireplace,' Oscar Browning tells us. 'Those who wished to converse with the great authoress whom they had come to visit took their seats in turns at the chair by her side.' Lewes moved about among the guests and poured tea. There are many accounts of George Eliot giving individual counsel to her admirers. Mrs Field, an American lady, tells us:

> A few words, and all reserve was gone. 'Come, sit by me on this sofa,' she said; and instantly, seated side by side, we were deep in conversation .... never did a sweeter voice fascinate a listener, — so soft and low that one must almost bend to hear. You can imagine what it was thus to sit for an hour beside this gifted woman and hear talk of questions interesting to the women of England and America .... While there is no attempt to impress you with her intellectual superiority, you naturally feel elevated into a higher sphere. The conversation itself floats upward into a region above the commonplace.

So it goes on and on; this is a typical report, in that we never get down to what was actually said. After a series of visits in 1872 and 73 Anny Thackeray said that she found the atmosphere *'too precious* at the *shrine*, and the cult of the *divinity* too oppressive ... There is a want of reality in it....'

One suspects Lewes's hand in all this. George Eliot was made to appear as a walking and talking parody of the Victorian sage. He seems to have forgotten that his wife was a writer, and not equipped to be a performer like himself. It was not easy to act out the rôle of Great Woman, and nothing in her earlier years had prepared her for such dignities; what did Robert Evans's daughter really think? What would Mrs Poyser have given vent to, if she had been able to have her say?

It seems kindest to suggest that George Eliot was still a very shy person who was unable to cope naturally with the public demands of her fame. There are many instances of her personal interest in younger people, and her kindness to those in real distress, which serve to cancel out some of the more ludicrous aspects of her behaviour. She was also blessed with a grown-up family of three boys; though she had no children of her own, she became a mother to Lewes's. In addition, it was her money which provided for Agnes Lewes.

As she grew older she grew more conservative in her political views. There is nothing unusual in this, but in her case there are baffling inconsistencies. For example, *Felix Holt* (1866) is subtitled *The Radical*; the novel combines a profound rejection of gentry and money values with a disconcertingly hostile attitude to the aspirations of working people. The next year 'Felix Holt' produced an 'Address to Working Men' on the occasion of the second Reform Act; though attempts have been made to praise the wisdom of this little tract, it is shot through with middle-class fears and prejudices. Yet the same mind was to go on to create the acutely observed political world of *Middlemarch*, and to end the novel with Dorothea married to an MP who is 'ardent' in the cause of Reform.

What is really baffling, as the epigraph to this section indicates so well, is that there is so little in George Eliot's last twenty years that one can point to as having 'the solidity of objects', to use her own phrase again, in relation to her character and ideas. There are masses of letters, and countless references to her in journals and diaries, but in the end she eludes us so completely. I therefore make no apology for only picking out one or two items for comment in the next few pages.

Music and poetry

> Not that her enjoyment of music was of the kind that indicates a great specific talent: it was rather that her sensibility to the supreme excitement of music was only one form of that passionate sensibility which belonged to her whole nature....
> *The Mill on the Floss*, Bk 6, Ch. 6, p. 514

George Eliot's own enjoyment of music may be quite fairly compared to this description of Maggie's ecstasy; it may also be considered appropriate for one born upon St Cecilia's day. The young Mary Ann Evans was given lessons at school and at home; a fellow-pupil said that it was the opinion of her teachers that 'she might make a performer equal to any then upon the public stage'. While at school in Coventry she was taught by the organist of St Michael's, Edward Simms; she also attended oratorios which he conducted. His excellence as a musician may well have led her to insert in *Middlemarch* the statement that Rosamond's master

> was one of those excellent musicians here and there to be found in our provinces, worthy to compare with many a noted Kapellmeister in a country which offers more plentiful conditions of musical celebrity.
> Ch. 16 p. 190

The forms and practice of music which had been encouraged in her childhood remained with her. Her ability to play classical sonatas on the piano, and also to accompany singers and other instrumentalists, enabled her to describe such musical performances in her novels, so that even Rosamond Vincy is redeemed by her 'large rendering of noble music' (p. 190). Similarly, the taste for large-scale oratorios never left her; she attended performances of the *Messiah*, and once heard *Elijah* conducted by Mendelssohn himself. When Herbert Spencer was music critic for *The Economist* he took her to a performance of *The Creation*. Wherever George Eliot travelled she managed to attend oratorios, or to form groups for the domestic enjoyment of music in the traditional Victorian manner.

Her taste for opera came later, when she had finally broken with prejudices of the English Midlands. Her first opera in London seems to have been *I Puritani*, an Italian romance upon the English Civil War, but after her union with G. H. Lewes she went frequently to opera and to concerts, hearing the music of Berlioz and Wagner, and on one occasion joining Liszt for breakfast. The growth in her musical taste and range is reflected in her novels; for example, the heroine of 'Mr Gilfil's Love-Story' is a singer, and a number of Italian songs are referred to. Hetty's attractiveness to Adam is compared to 'exquisite music', and Maggie's sensitivity to music is surely George Eliot's own.

The symbolic use of music in her novels is best illustrated from *The Mill on the Floss*, though this symbolism is rooted in actual descriptions of performance. In one of the scenes that precede the elopement Maggie's soul is played on by 'the inexorable power of sound' (Bk 6, Ch. 7, p. 532). Philip is trying to woo her through an aria from Bellini's *Sonnambula*—which is misspelt *Somnambula* in the manuscript and all early texts: 'the tenor is telling the heroine that he shall always love her though she may forsake him.' This application of the chosen song is entirely clear, but the sense of aimless sleepwalking and irresponsible automatism characterises Maggie throughout the ensuing sequence where she is gliding down the river and unable to call a halt to the compromising relationship. This prophetic use of music is confirmed when Stephen sings a more masculine ditty, 'and Maggie, in spite of her resistance to the spirit of the song and to the singer, was taken hold of and shaken by the invisible influence—was borne along by a wave too strong for her;' the later chapter in which this theme is developed is appropriately called "Borne along by the tide". Finally, at the end of this musical party, the group are unable to make a harmonious rendering of the music of *The Tempest*, a story with a clear reference to water and drowning, but which of course has a happier ending.

In *Daniel Deronda* Gwendolen Harleth, who aspires to become a professional musician, encounters Herr Klesmer, who may be said to represent one of the great travelling virtuosi of the day. Chapter 23 contains a description of the interview in which Klesmer dissuades her from becoming a professional and in doing so explains what he means by a 'real artist'. Klesmer has been thought by some to have been founded upon Liszt, while others have preferred his Russian rival, Anton Rubinstein. There are many other references to music in the Zionist part of this novel, both to the actual singing of Mirah, and, more deeply symbolical, to musical analogies for the extension of consciousness which the prophet Mordecai seems capable of.

This deeper meaning of music was constantly present to George Eliot, particularly in her poetry. This largely forgotten body of work seems to have occupied her during the late 1860s, when her novel-writing seemed temporarily to have ceased. *The Spanish Gypsy* contains a wealth of musical imagery, which is intended to describe relations between unawakened souls, and the interspersed lyrics in this poetic drama have a surprising intensity. In this example the imagery of embarkation and exploration is juxtaposed with frightening consequences:

> Push off the boat,
>   Quit, quit the shore,
>   The stars will guide us back:—
> O gathering cloud,
>   O wide, wide sea,
>   O waves that keep no track!
>
> On through the pines!
>   The pillared woods,
>   Where silence breathes sweet breath:—
> O labyrinth,
>   O sunless gloom,
>   The other side of death!

The most familiar of her poems draws upon the ancient mystical and Platonic idea that there is an angelic music of the spheres, and proposes a 'Positivist' view of continuing life after death. Such is the power of the musical imagery that it is very difficult not to believe in the 'choir invisible'; the poem creates an idea of a future life which overwhelms the Positivist negation of it:

> O may I join the choir invisible
> Of those immortal dead who live again
> In minds made better by their presence....
>   This is life to come,
> Which martyred men have made more glorious
> For us who strive to follow. May I reach
> That purest heaven, be to other souls
> The cup of strength in some great agony,
> Enkindle generous ardour, feed pure love,
> Beget the smiles that have no cruelty—

> Be the sweet presence of a good diffused,
> And in diffusion ever more intense.
> So shall I join the choir invisible
> Whose music is the gladness of the world.

These examples of her devotion to music and poetry as a way of expressing her inner life do, I think, help to build up a more convincing picture of George Eliot than the public image of her later years. It is worth pointing out that in fact her last public appearance was at a Saturday Pop Concert in St James's Hall; she insisted on attending this in spite of the onset of illness, and though many of the audience may have considered her to be more important than the performers, her own attention was given to the music.

Finale

> We may be thankful that she had found a good husband and a *Name*, it comforts me to know that she who for so many years was believed to be the wife of Lewes, had not Mary Ann Evans inscribed on her coffin.
>
> Letter to Isaac Evans from his half-sister Fanny, 1881

In 1876, after a long search, the Leweses invested money in the purchase of a country house at Witley in Surrey. They were helped in this transaction by Johnny Cross, a young friend who had become their banker. One of the reasons for choosing a quiet country residence was that Lewes was in poor health; but he kept up such a show of *bonhomie* that it was not apparent that he was dying until November 1878. They returned to The Priory where Lewes died on the 30th of the same month; he had been suffering from cancer of the bowel. Marian tried to persuade herself that he had been unaware that death was upon him. She could not bring herself to attend the funeral as she was so deeply affected. Her friends escorted the body to Highgate Cemetery, where Lewes was buried in unconsecrated ground.

In 1879 Blackwood made sure that she finished the volume of essays by 'Theophrastus Such'; she also laboured to complete her husband's *Problems of Life and Mind*. After a while she allowed herself to resume her friendship with Johnny Cross, and received some comfort from her many female friends and admirers. Nevertheless, she surprised everybody by her marriage to Cross in May 1880. Isaac wrote to congratulate his sister on the 'happy event which has been communicated to me'—after a silence of twenty-three years.

The honeymoon was enlivened by the bridegroom's leaping from the balcony of his hotel bedroom: luckily it was in Venice, and he came to no harm in the Grand Canal. On their return, the newly married couple spent the summer at Witley. In December they were able to move into a new London house in Cheyne Walk, but a severe kidney infection, which had appeared to be simply 'a sore throat', took Marian by surprise—she became seriously ill, and died on the 22nd. The rapidity of all this shocked her friends; Anny Thackeray, who was not particularly close to her, commented:

> It is absurd, but I do feel George Eliot's death very much. There is nothing to be sorry for—all is at peace for her, poor soul, but it haunts one somehow. She was buried in a great storm of wind and rain or I think I should have gone to the funeral.

It was decided to bury her near to Lewes's grave at Highgate; the best account of the funeral is that of Edith Simcox. She had been one of George Eliot's more fervent disciples, and had had to be rebuked on one occasion for kissing her beloved's feet; but in most other matters she was a discerning and capable woman. This is the entry in her diary:

WEDNESDAY 29 DECEMBER 1880

29. This day stands alone. I am not afraid of forgetting, but as heretofore I record her teaching while the sound is still fresh in my soul's ears. This morning at 10 when the wreath I had ordered—white flowers bordered with laurel leaves—came, I drove with it to Cheyne Walk, giving it silently to the silent cook. Then, instinct guiding—it seemed to guide one right all day—I went to Highgate, stopping on the way to get some violets—I was not sure for what purpose. In the cemetery I found the new grave was in the place I had feebly coveted—nearer the path than his and one step further south. Then I laid my violets at the head of Mr. Lewes's solitary grave and left the already gathering crowd to ask which way the entrance would be. Then I drifted towards the chapel—standing first for a while under the colonnade where a child asked me 'Was it the late George Eliot's wife was going to be buried?'—I think I said Yes. Then I waited on the skirts of the group gathered in the porch between the church and chapel sanctuaries. Then some one claimed a passage through the thickening crowd and I followed in his wake and found myself without effort in a sort of vestibule past the door which kept back the crowd. Mrs. Lankester was next the chapel—I cannot forget that she offered me her place. I took it and presently every one else was made to stand back, then the solemn procession passed me. The coffin bearers paused in the very doorway, I pressed a kiss upon the pall and trembled violently as I stood motionless else, in the still silence with nothing to mar the realization of that intense moment's awe. Then—it was hard to tell the invited mourners from the other waiting

friends—men many of whose faces I knew—and so I passed among them into the chapel, entering a forward pew. White wreaths lay thick upon the velvet pall—it was not painful to think of her last sleep so guarded. I saw her husband's face, pale and still; he forced himself aloof from the unbearable world in sight. The service was so like our own I did not know it apart till afterwards when I could not trace the outlines that had seemed so almost entirely in harmony with her faith. Dr. Sadler quoted— how could he help?—her words of aspiration, but what moved me most was the passage—in the Church Service lesson—it moved me like the voice of God—of Her: 'But some man will say, How are the dead raised up? and with what body do they come?' ... As we left the chapel Miss Helps put her arm in mine, but I left her at the door, to make my way alone across the road to the other part where the grave was. I shook hands silently with Mrs. Anderson and waited at the corner where the hearse stopped and the coffin was brought up again. Again I followed near, on the skirts of the procession, a man—Champneys I thought—had a white wreath he wished to lay upon the coffin and as he pressed forward those behind bore me on, till I was standing between his grave and hers and heard the last words said: the grave was deep and narrow—the flowers filled all the level space. I turned away with the first—Charles Lewes pressed my hand as we gave the last look. Then I turned up the hill and walked through the rain by a road unknown before to Hampstead and a station. Then through the twilight I cried and moaned aloud.

Letters, IX 323–4

The idea of a future life

> The human nature unto which I felt
> That I belonged, and reverenced with love,
> Was not a punctual presence, but a spirit
> Diffused through time and space ....
> Wordsworth, *The Prelude*, quoted in *Daniel Deronda*

In following the development of George Eliot's novels from 'Amos Barton' to *Daniel Deronda*, we shall notice changes in the tone of the discussion of religion, and these are heightened if we go even further back in a general retrospect. The young firebrand of the 1850s, who had slaughtered the Evangelicals in the person of Dr Cumming and terminated the high reputation of the glib poet Edward Young, had rapidly become more tolerant of other people's beliefs. Consider the letter she wrote in 1859 to M. D'Albert Durade, whom she had not seen since 1849–50:

> Ten years of experience have wrought great changes in that inward self: I have no longer any antagonism towards any faith in

which human sorrow and human longing for purity have expressed themselves....

I have not returned to dogmatic Christianity ... but I see in it the highest expression of the religious sentiment that has yet found its place in the history of mankind.... Many things that I should have argued against ten years ago, I now feel myself too ignorant and too limited in moral sensibility to speak of with confident disapprobation: on many points where I used to delight in expressing intellectual difference, I now delight in feeling an emotional agreement.

Letters, III 230–1

By November 1862 she is able to say to write to Barbara Bodichon that she has 'lost all interest in mere antagonism to religious doctrines.'

And the Religion of Humanity? This of course was a term of special meaning to the Comtists, who continually urged her to join them; this she was reluctant to do, nor would she help them by composing a 'Liturgy' for their use (Haight p. 506). They were particularly shocked when she married in 1880, for this was a direct rejection of the Comtean belief in perpetual widowhood.

The most famous account of her later beliefs is that of F. W. H. Myers:

> I remember how, at Cambridge, I walked with her once in the Fellows' Garden of Trinity, on an evening of rainy May; and she, stirred somewhat beyond her wont, and taking as her text the three words which have been used so often as the inspiring trumpet-calls of men,—the words *God, Immortality, Duty*,—pronounced, with terrible earnestness, how inconceivable was the *first*, how unbelievable the *second*, and yet how peremptory and absolute the *third*. Never, perhaps, have sterner accents affirmed the sovereignty of impersonal and unrecompensing Law. I listened, and night fell; her grave, majestic countenance turned towards me like a Sibyl's in the gloom; it was as though she withdrew from my grasp, one by one, the two scrolls of promise, and left me the third scroll only, awful with inevitable fates. And when we stood at length and parted, amid that columnar circuit of the forest-trees, beneath the last twilight of starless skies, I seemed to be gazing, like Titus at Jerusalem, on vacant seats and empty halls,—on a sanctuary with no Presence to hallow it, and heaven left lonely of a God.

This is so well written, some might say overwritten, that it has become entwined with our general over-quick reactions to the spot question: 'What did George Eliot actually believe?' As Haight points out in his discussion of the passage, Myers goes on to qualify this extreme account (Haight p. 465).

Myers would have disagreed with her about the second proposition because he was a Spiritualist; George Eliot was not attracted to this doctrine, though she did attend a séance with G. H. Lewes. In fact, one of the things which distinguished her from others in the nineteenth century who lost their faith was that she did not flirt with each and every new substitute for religion which came her way. Yet there is one thread which binds together all the stages of her religious development, and that is her interest in the idea of the future life. One of the books which she read in the 1830s while sorting out her religious beliefs was Isaac Taylor's *Physical Theory of Another Life* (1836). The author indulged in daring speculations; so did Marian Evans. She dabbled in Pantheistic beliefs, and a book to be called *The Idea of a Future Life* was 'announced' with her translation of Feuerbach in 1853. Feuerbach indeed has a very good chapter on this topic, and made her see that the projection of a future life was really the desire to perpetuate the good things of our present existence. As she indicated in the letter to Durade which has already been quoted from:

> On that question of our future existence, to which you allude, I have undergone the sort of change I have just indicated, although my most rooted conviction is, that the immediate objects and the proper sphere of all our highest emotions are our struggling fellowmen and this earthly existence.

There remains, therefore, some considerable doubt as to her final position on this matter. We have noticed that her poem 'O may I join the choir invisible', written in 1867, proposed a subjective view of immortality, which was enhanced by the musical imagery in which she clothed her deepest feelings. *Middlemarch* confines itself strictly to observations about this world, but by the mid-seventies the extraordinary change of emphasis in *Daniel Deronda* cannot be ignored. It is true that by then developments in scientific theory, particularly in physics, had begun to undermine the former certainties on which the Positivists had based their rejection of metaphysics, and the new ideas in *Daniel Deronda* are pushed beyond the frontier of the rational and materialist position which George Eliot had formerly been supposed to uphold. When Mordecai dies, he prophesies that his soul will live on in Daniel Deronda, and more than a cliché is to be inferred; the conclusion may be that individual souls will be subsumed in the 'future life' of the race. Speculation can go no further; it is the unwritten books of authors which continue to haunt them, as opposed to those in which they have finally settled issues with themselves. *The Idea of a Future Life* must remain in that category, a text awaiting an author, a book to construct for ourselves.

Part Two
Critical Survey

Note

This survey consists of a number of short essays, interspersed with a series of prose extracts taken from George Eliot's works: The extracts are in each case followed by analytical notes. Apart from 'Amos Barton' and *Romola*, which are comparatively unfamiliar texts, I have not attempted to re-tell the story of any novel. The first essays deal with more than one work, comparing and contrasting characters and themes: it is expected that the reader will turn to these while studying a particular novel. The general emphasis of this survey is an attempt to show how the earlier stories prepare us for *Middlemarch*, and how *Daniel Deronda* departs from it.

6 'The Natural History of German Life'

George Eliot's essays for the *Westminster Review* and other periodicals may seem an unpromising field for criticism. They were frequently written to order, but as she became more experienced she was able to choose her own subjects. A careful reading of her essays reveals many passages which anticipate the interests of the novelist; indeed, in some of her descriptions of her travels in Germany we tremble on the verge of her fictional style.

She was also in demand as reviewer of German books, and in May 1856 she produced a long article about the work of Wilhelm Heinrich von Riehl, who might be described a pioneer anthropologist; he concerned himself with the life of the German peasant; she described his most recent book *Land und Leute* (Land and People) as 'fascinating as literature, if it were not important for its facts and philosophy'.

Her review begins by examining the relation between the 'language' of sociology, art and literature, and the people they purport to observe. This is seen to be seriously askew, and she explains that even Holman Hunt, 'one of the greatest painters of the pre-eminently realistic school, while, in his picture of "The Hireling Shepherd", he gave us a landscape of marvellous truthfulness, placed a pair of peasants in the foreground who were not much more real than the idyllic swains and damsels of our chimney ornaments.' The artist cannot see the peasants for what they really are, and this failure of perception is also to be seen in the English novelists, to whom the discussion then turns: 'our social novels profess to represent the people as they are, and the unreality of their representations is a grave evil.' Von Riehl's careful observation of the German peasantry should be taken as a model, conscious as he is of local differences, peculiarities of dialect and the living history which the peasants body forth; he notes their adherence to time-honoured custom as 'the supreme law', and sees that in this way they keep the past alive without knowing what they do. In these matters George Eliot can only compare von Riehl's insight with that of the novelist Sir Walter Scott; Scott is frequently brought into the discussion, and praised in contrast to the English novelists who 'transfer their own feelings to ploughmen and woodcutters, and give them both joys and sorrows of which they know nothing'.

In fact, the article has begun to slide away from von Riehl into a discussion of the practice of novel-writing, and George Eliot contri-

butes her own description of a haymaking scene, which might find a place in *Adam Bede*. In the second part of her article she returns to a discussion of von Riehl's main ideas; his patient collecting of material from all over Germany before coming to conclusions shows the thoroughness of his approach. There are reflections on the nature of language, and a picture of European society as 'incarnate history': this is the section from which the following extract is taken. Social Science—referring to Herbert Spencer, Auguste Comte and other systematisers of the time—Social Science is empty theory compared to 'the Natural History of Social Bodies'. This is what is now needed in the study of human beings. George Eliot concludes with a salute to 'the conservatism of a clear-eyed, practical, but withal large-minded man'—a compliment which we could later turn to use about George Eliot herself, especially when we see her putting von Riehl's theory into the writing of her own novels.

Prose extract: The historical conditions of society . . .

> The historical conditions of society may be compared with those of language. It must be admitted that the language of cultivated nations is in anything but a rational state; the great sections of the civilized world are only approximately intelligible to each other, and even that, only at the cost of long study; one word stands for many things, and many words for one thing; the subtle shades of meaning, and still subtler echoes of association, make language an instrument which scarcely anything short of genius can wield with definiteness and certainty. Suppose, then, that the effort which has been again and again made to construct a universal language on a rational basis has at length succeeded, and that you have a language which has no uncertainty, no whims of idiom, no cumbrous forms, no fitful shimmer of many-hued significance, no hoary archaisms 'familiar with forgotten years'— a patent de-odorized and non-resonant language, which effects the purpose of communication as perfectly and rapidly as algebraic signs. Your language may be a perfect medium of expression to science, but will never express *life*, which is a great deal more than science. With the anomalies and inconveniences of historical language, you will have parted with its music and its passion, with its vital qualities as an expression of individual character, with its subtle capabilities of wit, with everything that gives it power over the imagination; and the next step in simplification will be the invention of a talking watch, which will achieve the utmost facility and dispatch in the communication of

The Hireling Shepherd *by William Holman Hunt, 1851*

ideas by a graduated adjustment of ticks, to be represented in writing by a corresponding arrangement of dots. A melancholy 'language of the future!' The sensory and motor nerves that run in the same sheath, are scarcely bound together by a more necessary and delicate union than that which binds men's affection, imagination, wit, and humour, with the subtle ramifications of historical language. Language must be left to grow in precision, completeness, and unity, as minds grow in clearness, comprehensiveness, and sympathy. And there is an analogous relation between the moral tendencies of men and the social conditions they have inherited. The nature of European men has its roots intertwined with the past, and can only be developed by allowing those roots to remain undisturbed while the process of development is going on, until that perfect ripeness of the seed which carries with it a life independent of the root. This vital connexion with the past is much more vividly felt on the Continent than in England, where we have to recall it by an effort of memory and reflection; for though our English life is in its core intensely traditional, Protestantism and commerce have modernized the face of the land and the aspects of society in a far greater degree than in any continental country:

> Abroad, [says Ruskin], a building of the eighth or tenth century stands ruinous in the open street; the children play round it, the peasants heap their corn in it, the buildings of yesterday nestle about it, and fit their new stones in its rents, and tremble in sympathy as it trembles. No one wonders at it, or thinks of it as separate, and of another time; we feel the ancient world to be a real thing, and one with the new; antiquity is no dream; it is rather the children playing about the old stones that are the dream. But all is continuous; and the words 'from generation to generation', understandable here.
>
> *Essays* pp. 287–9

PROSE STYLE Victorian prose may well seem 'heavier' than modern English, especially because punctuation conventions are more formal. There are long sentences contained in this very long single paragraph, in which even the little piece of Ruskin at the end could easily be thought of as a paragraph on its own in a more modern essay. It may also be that George Eliot has picked up the convention of the long paragraph from translating German, where it is more usual.

The way in which George Eliot handles the paragraph seems at first a model of rationality. The first sentence marks out clearly what is to be done: A is to be compared to B. In fact the comparison ('Language') takes up over half of the paragraph, and we can see that the idea within it has excited the author to superfluity of expression ('no ... no ... no ...' etc.). With the words 'And there is an analogous relation', the author returns us to the main subject under discussion: the connection of society with its past. A series of statements, using rather hackneyed imagery—'roots' and 'core', leads us to the drabness of English life, which is splendidly off-set by the piece of prose-poetry from Ruskin.

THE ARGUMENT In the same way that a totally constructed and artificial language, of the kind frequently demanded by scientists for example, would be deprived of historical resonances, so a totally new society would be similarly lacking in history and men's 'moral tendencies' would be without foundation. The risk to the 'moral tendencies' does not seem to follow logically from the foregoing argument, since it was not clear that language had moral overtones, 'affection ... sympathy', until the last two sentences of the language section, beginning with 'The sensory and motor nerves'. In fact, the whole sequence of thought is emotional, and not the logical structure which it first appeared to be; it resembles the arguments about the development of the moral sense in poets like Wordsworth, and the piece of Ruskin is like the 'beautiful passages' in Wordsworth's *Prelude*.

POLITICS The direction of the thinking might be described as pretty 'conservative': it is best to leave old institutions alone. Since it is an account of von Riehl's thinking it might be said to be his idea rather than hers. But her liberal mind is in sympathy with it, and the words 'process of development', although a cliché today, can be taken to refer to the Development Theory, an earlier version of the Theory of Evolution, which Herbert Spencer and similar thinkers were rather daringly propagating in the 1850s; 'as minds grow in clearness, comprehensiveness and sympathy' combines phrenological overtones (bigger brains are better) with the Idea of Progress ('These things shall be: a loftier race' etc.). Nevertheless, the fascination with the past is what comes across; she approves of von Riehl's 'incarnate history'. The two strands in her thinking, the liberal progressive, and the conservative or even 'Tory' reactionary, can be seen debating within her in this single paragraph. This debate will continue in her novels, and I don't myself see the gap that others detect between her journalism and her fictional work.

LOOKING TO THE FUTURE Haight said "The article is one of the richest she ever wrote. In it we see her mind turning back to the memories of her childhood among the common people of Warwickshire with the vivid sympathy that was soon to flower in her fiction. Anyone who wishes to understand the origin of George Eliot's novels should read the essay on Riehl." This general judgement is borne out by several points of detail. There is a discussion of how

Hetty's face 'transcended her feelings' in Chapter 26 of *Adam Bede* (p. 330); it speaks 'the joys and sorrows of foregone generations ... just as a national language may be instinct with poetry unfelt by the lips that use it.' The Wordsworth phrase 'familiar with forgotten years' (*Excursion*, I, 276) will be used again in the description of St Ogg's in *The Mill on the Floss* (Bk I, Ch. 12, pp. 181–2). But in the same novel there is also the oppressiveness of a peasant society—'the religion of the Dodsons'—and its effect upon those who try to break free from it. Peter Coveney, in his introduction to the Penguin edition of *Felix Holt*, sees the essay on von Riehl as an anticipation of the Author's Introduction to that novel; he also sees it as leading directly to 'Shepperton Church', which is the next extract we consider. It is the beginning of her first story, 'The Sad Fortunes of the Rev. Amos Barton'.

Prose extract: Shepperton Church

SHEPPERTON Church was a very different-looking building five-and-twenty years ago. To be sure, its substantial stone tower looks at you through its intelligent eye, the clock, with the friendly expression of former days; but in everything else what changes! Now there is a wide span of slated roof flanking the old steeple; the windows are tall and symmetrical; the outer doors are resplendent with oak-graining, the inner doors reverentially noiseless with a garment of red baize; and the walls, you are convinced, no lichen will ever again effect a settlement on—they are smooth and innutrient as the summit of the Rev. Amos Barton's head, after ten years of baldness and supererogatory soap. Pass through the baize doors and you will see the nave filled with well-shaped benches, understood to be free seats; while in certain eligible corners, less directly under the fire of the clergyman's eye, there are pews reserved for the Shepperton gentility. Ample galleries are supported on iron pillars, and in one of them stands the crowning glory, the very clasp or aigrette of Shepperton church-adornment—namely, an organ, not very much out of repair, on which a collector of small rents, differentiated by the force of circumstances into an organist, will accompany the alacrity of your departure after the blessing, by a sacred minuet or an easy 'Gloria'.

Immense improvement! says the well-regulated mind, which unintermittingly rejoices in the New Police, the Tithe Commutation Act, the penny-post, and all guarantees of human advance-

Chilvers Coton Church, engraving from the Illustrated London News, *1881. Though this shows the church after restoration, 'a little flight of steps with a wooden rail' can be seen to the left.*

ment, and has no moments when conservative-reforming intellect takes a nap, while imagination does a little Toryism by the sly, revelling in regret that dear, old, brown, crumbling, picturesque inefficiency is everywhere giving place to spick-and-span new-painted, new-varnished efficiency, which will yield endless diagrams, plans, elevations, and sections, but alas! no picture. Mine, I fear, is not a well-regulated mind: it has an occasional tenderness for old abuses; it lingers with a certain fondness over the days of nasal clerks and top-booted parsons, and has a sigh for the departed shades of vulgar errors. So it is not surprising that I recall with a fond sadness Shepperton Church as it was in the old days, with its outer coat of rough stucco, its red-tiled roof, its heterogeneous windows patched with desultory bits of painted glass, and its little flight of steps with their wooden rail running up the outer wall, and leading to the school-children's gallery.

Scenes of Clerical Life, pp. 41–2

FIRST IMPRESSIONS This is the first page of George Eliot's fiction, yet how much it sounds like the opening of an essay. It also expands upon the point made in the article on the work of von Riehl. The contrast in the first extract between deodorised universal language and that containing archaisms 'familiar with forgotten years' is repeated in the regret shown in these paragraphs for the demise of the old church and the distaste for 'the well-regulated mind'. This is made abundantly evident in the praise of old-fashioned Toryism, which is carefully distinguished from the 'conservative reforms' of Peel and his followers. These sentiments would surely have surprised anybody who knew the Liberal journalist Marian Evans; perhaps she is deliberately laying a false trail.

TONE There is a considerable difference from the tone of the first extract. In that passage we were being lectured at, explained to, asked to agree with a reasonable argument. Here there is much more irony; in almost every sentence there are examples. The *thing* discussed—i.e. the new church, the *utterance* of 'the well-regulated mind', and even the *reader*, who is addressed as 'you'—all are played with, picked up and dropped. It is like the proverbial cat making game of a helpless mouse. This is a writer who loves to tease. Nevertheless, there is also a warmth present—'tenderness ... lingers ... fond sadness'—which is almost like the old varnish presumably referred to in 'dear, old, brown, crumbling ...' and so on.

FUNCTION The passage serves as a prologue to two of the *Scenes of Clerical Life* in which the church is featured. The thoughts about church-restoration were very topical in the 1850s, as was the consciousness that something had been lost in the process, which might be described as the organic link to the past. This is why the opening announcement of a gap of twenty-five years is so important: the past has gone for good, and has been cleaned away, or cleaned up, like the old church. And so we can contemplate the past as separate or distant from us; it seems at first that we will not get sentimentally involved in trying to recall it. But such is the power of memory that by the end of the second paragraph the church has been reconstructed in its original picturesque muddle.

The device of beginning with the description of a building and sliding into an account of the people who have used or inhabited it is not uncommon; it is a favourite trick of the meandering periodical essayist. 'The Old Benchers of the Inner Temple', by Charles Lamb, might well be the unconscious model for this opening of a story. Her other early novels will begin with a similar slide; after 'the Egyptian blot' we first see the interior of the carpenter's workshop in *Adam Bede*, the opening chapter of *The Mill on the Floss* is concerned with the view from a bridge, and *Romola* commences with a vision of the old city of Florence. As G.H. Lewes observed, she is good at description, but can she manage drama?

PROSE STYLE It reads well aloud. It seems to be written for the speaking voice; in fact she did read most of her work out loud to Lewes. Each paragraph begins the new topic with a short announcement, but soon begins to go back on itself and to wind about. Notice how the last sentence of the first paragraph keeps on branching and growing; it would naturally have come to an end much earlier, but the writer will not let the joke go or the reader depart. Similarly, the last sentence of the second paragraph is mimetic, with the long clause about 'the little flight of steps' seeming to take you with it up those steps, and leading you, the reader, and George Eliot, the writer, into the gallery with the schoolchildren. The next paragraph will present the church through the eyes of one of the children, who is the author herself, gone back into the past.

CONCLUSION The key phrase remains 'while imagination does a little Toryism by the sly'. Though we have noted the ironical pose, what exactly is the relation of intellect to imagination in this mental dialogue? Is it the case that imagination is not to be trusted out of sight of the intellect? Do we identify the intellect with Marian Evans the journalist, and the imagination with George Eliot the novelist? I would not like to go as far as this, as I see the 'author' of this passage as resembling so closely the 'author' of the passage from the article on von Riehl; but her voice has gained in confidence. The intellect is established as the imperceptive and dozy component of her ill-regulated mind, and is finally put to sleep; the narrator has decided to follow the imagination wherever it may lead her.

7 The transformation of reality: 'Amos Barton' to *Adam Bede*

George Eliot's first efforts at fiction were originally published as separate stories in *Blackwood's Magazine*; in 1858 they were issued in volume form with the title *Scenes of Clerical Life*. Although the title may seem quite unprepossessing, it would have interested readers who had followed the spate of religious novels through the 1840s; few of these are now remembered. On the whole they were novels which dealt with religious questions, and, most seriously, doubt and the loss of faith. These are matters on which it might be expected that George Eliot would have had something to say; in fact the reverse is the case. The fundamentals of the Christian religion were neither doubted nor discussed in George Eliot's stories. Their aims were revealed in a letter from G. H. Lewes to Blackwood accompanying the first of the series: they were to be

> tales and sketches illustrative of the actual life of our country clergy about a quarter of a century ago; but solely in its *human* and *not at all* in its *theological* aspect; the object being to do what has never been done in our literature, for we have had abundant religious stories polemical and doctrinal, but since the 'Vicar' and Miss Austen, no stories representing the clergy like any other class with the humours, sorrows, and troubles of other men.
>
> *Letters*, II 269

(The 'Vicar' refers to Oliver Goldsmith's *The Vicar of Wakefield*.) On the whole, this seems rather a large claim in that Trollope's *The Warden* had carried out a similar programme when it appeared in 1855, but George Eliot and Lewes appear not to have read it.

The reference to Jane Austen is also worth noting. Appreciation of her work was very 'patchy' in the nineteenth century, and she was usually underestimated. Earlier in the 1850s George Eliot had written in an article on 'Lady Novelists':

> First and foremost let Jane Austen be named, the greatest artist that has ever written. . . . Life, as it appears to an English gentlewoman peacefully yet actively engaged in her quiet village, is mirrored in her works. . . . To read one of her books is like an actual experience of life.

This may help us to understand the intentions of George Eliot in the *Scenes of Clerical Life*—to reproduce the effect of life itself; the word 'Scenes' was originally 'Sketches', implying an unfinished or literal account as opposed to a worked-up or finished production. It means what Katherine Mansfield was later to call 'the slice of life'.

The first story, which is called 'The Sad Fortunes of the Rev. Amos Barton', fits this description exactly. There is no plot, and none of the contrivances of 'fiction'; things just happen. It was close to life because it was about the misfortunes of a real clergyman, the Rev. John Gwyther, curate of Chilvers Coton from 1831 to 1841. George Eliot presumably thought he was dead, and was rather surprised when, after reading the story, the unfortunate cleric wrote in to *Blackwood's Magazine*. We must not allow this fact to divert us from the theory of literature which the story is trying to exemplify; it does not matter that Gwyther recognised himself, or that his wife's tomb may be seen in Chilvers Coton churchyard. If George Eliot had only been capable of copying from life, the result would have been trivial or meaningless. What we are concerned with is George Eliot's art: this story is deliberately written about a real person, not because she had no imagination, but because she was trying to put into practice the principles she had inculcated in the essay on von Riehl; furthermore, it is deliberately written as an anti-story or a non-story, that is to say it is written *against literature*, in the same way that some of Wordsworth's *Lyrical Ballads* were intended to shock people out of literary convention by intruding real people upon their consideration.

The tale of Amos Barton is extremely simple in outline: he is a poor curate of Evangelical views, with a loving wife and six children; people sneer at him behind his back, particularly when he is taken up by an unsuitable patroness, a so-called Countess, who finds herself short of money and takes up residence in the vicarage; when she finally does depart, his wife dies in childbirth; at this point the common humanity of the parishioners overcomes their initial distaste for the curate; but it is to no avail, because he is forced to leave the parish too, when the curacy is reassigned by the absentee vicar to his brother-in-law. As George Eliot announces at the beginning of Chapter 5, when she is beginning to get round to telling the story:

> The Rev. Amos Barton, whose sad fortunes I have undertaken to relate, was, you perceive, in no respect an ideal or exceptional character; and perhaps I am doing a bold thing to bespeak your sympathy on behalf of a man who was so very far from remarkable,—a man whose virtues were not heroic, and who had no undetected crime within his breast; who had not the slightest mystery hanging about him, but was palpably and unmistakably commonplace; who was not even in love, but had had that complaint favourably many years ago. 'An utterly uninteresting

character!' I think I hear a lady reader exclaim—Mrs Farthingale, for example, who prefers the ideal in fiction; to whom tragedy means ermine tippets, adultery, and murder; and comedy, the adventures of some personage who is quite a 'character'.

But, my dear madam, it is so very large a majority of your fellow-countrymen that are of this insignificant stamp. At least eighty out of a hundred of your adult male fellow-Britons returned in the last census are neither extraordinarily silly, nor extraordinarily wicked, nor extraordinarily wise; their eyes are neither deep and liquid with sentiment, nor sparkling with suppressed witticisms; they have probably had no hairbreadth escapes or thrilling adventures; their brains are certainly not pregnant with genius, and their passions have not manifested themselves at all after the fashion of a volcano. They are simply men of complexions more or less muddy, whose conversation is more or less bald and disjointed. Yet these commonplace people—many of them—bear a conscience, and have felt the sublime prompting to do the painful right; they have their unspoken sorrows, and their sacred joys; their hearts have perhaps gone out towards their first-born, and they have mourned over the irreclaimable dead. Nay, is there not a pathos in their very insignificance—in our comparison of their dim and narrow existence with the glorious possibilities of that human nature which they share?

Depend upon it, you would gain unspeakably if you would learn with me to see some of the poetry and the pathos, the tragedy and the comedy, lying in the experience of a human soul that looks out through dull grey eyes, and that speaks in a voice of quite ordinary tones. In that case, I should have no fear of your not caring to know what farther befell the Rev. Amos Barton, or of your thinking the homely details I have to tell at all beneath your attention. As it is, you can, if you please, decline to pursue my story farther; and you will easily find reading more to your taste, since I learn from the newspapers that many remarkable novels, full of striking situations, thrilling incidents, and eloquent writing, have appeared only within the last season.

pp. 80–1

This is exactly the same technique that Wordsworth had used in 'Simon Lee, the Old Huntsman, with an incident in which he was concerned'. The reader is first of all, as in a good Evangelical sermon, made to feel thoroughly ashamed of his or her sins in preferring 'exciting fiction'. Later on, George Eliot reiterates the point, this time with the irony at the reader's expense suddenly withdrawn:

> For not having a lofty imagination, as you perceive, and being unable to invent thrilling incidents for your amusement, my only merit must lie in the truth with which I represent to you the humble experience of ordinary fellow-mortals. I wish to stir your sympathy with commonplace troubles—to win your tears for real sorrow: sorrow such as may live next door to you—such as walks neither in rags nor in velvet, but in very ordinary decent apparel.
>
> p. 97

The story of Amos Barton is, in fact, extremely moving. The death of his wife Millie, with her children standing round the bed, could easily have been the 'tear-jerker' which we might have expected in a Victorian fiction. It is handled with extreme economy of effect. The narration is characterised by understatement throughout, and George Eliot does succeed in conveying the tragedy in ordinary people's lives. The sad little tale is leavened by humour; it is a rather brittle and waspish humour at times, and no doubt is meant to remind one of Jane Austen. It leads, however, to flashes of more earthy and proverbial wit, especially in the dialogue; Mr Hackit says of Amos:

> When he tries to preach wi'out book, he rambles about, and doesn't stick to his text; and every now and then he flounders about like a sheep as has cast itself, and can't get on its legs again.
>
> p. 48

This looks forward to the sayings of Mrs Poyser in *Adam Bede*.

'Amos Barton' was, incidentally, T.S. Eliot's favourite George Eliot story. It can even be argued that it is the most 'modern' of her works, and perhaps the most courageous thing she ever wrote; thereafter she slides quite rapidly towards the more conventional fiction required of a Victorian novelist. Though this may seem a very unusual point of view, it certainly illuminates the other stories in the *Scenes of Clerical Life*. 'Mr Gilfil's Love-story' seems impossibly melodramatic and might, with its romantic love and tragic coincidence, be the work of a different writer; the climax, where the heroine resolves to kill her fickle lover with a dagger, but finds him already dead from a heart-attack, made even Blackwood demur. The redeeming feature of the story is the occasional humour, which is of the same kind as the preceding *Scene*; for example, Mrs Bellamy, the housekeeper, remarks of a portrait that it represents Sir Francis Bacon, 'who invented gunpowder and in her opinion "might ha' been better employed"' (p. 154). The third story, 'Janet's Repentance', is nominally about 'drink', but it of great value as a study of the impact of Evangelicalism on the town of Milby; it is based upon actual events in Nuneaton during her childhood, but she insisted to Blackwood that 'Everything is softened from the fact. . . .' With these rather ominous words in mind, we turn to what would have been the fourth story of the *Scenes*, had it not been decided to allow George Eliot the 'fuller canvas' of a three-volume novel.

The opening sentences of *Adam Bede* are not at all what we would expect from a 'realistic' writer:

> With a single drop of ink for a mirror, the Egyptian sorcerer undertakes to reveal to any chance comer far-reaching visions of the past. This is what I undertake to do for you, reader. With this drop of ink at the end of my pen I will show you. . . .

These exotic references to visions and sorcery might be intended to make 'the reader' shudder, and to anticipate the kind of story which the author of 'Amos Barton' was so scornful about, a Gothic fantasy or a tale of horror. Though there is an element of this sensationalism in the subject-matter, particularly in the crime committed by the unfortunate Hetty Sorrel, this is not the flavour that remains with us after reading the book. Perhaps the first sentences of the novel are, after all, a kind of joke, as the realist author soon tumbles us out into the consciousness of a 'rough grey shepherd dog', and we find ourselves lying on a pile of shavings in a carpenter's workshop. The 'past' turns out to be the 1790s, a fact of which the novelist occasionally reminds us by discreet references to *Lyrical Ballads*, for example. The distance in time seems to lend enchantment to the view, the pastoral idyll is frequently brought to mind, and the sights and scents of an English summer dominate our senses as we read on. Indeed, George Eliot wrote to Blackwood on 17 October 1857, when she had hardly started on the book, that it was to be 'full of the breath of cows and the scent of hay'.

The original germ of the novel was, once again, a true story, told to George Eliot by her aunt, Mrs Samuel Evans. (An expanded account of the trial and death of Mary Voce is to be found in the biographical section.) Mrs Evans had been a Methodist preacher. In the novel the scene-setting, the problems of Adam and Seth Bede, and the extensive treatment of the preaching of Dinah Morris, all seem to establish these characters at the centre of the story and to force Hetty and Arthur into the sub-plot: it takes a long time to get to the murder of the baby, particularly as the reader, like Adam himself, has to work out exactly what is wrong with Hetty in the first place. The tragic consequences are rushed through in the last third of the book. There is also an opposition between the pastoral and the melodramatic elements in the story which has disconcerted many readers; the last-minute rescue of Hetty seems very contrived, and there is a feeling of let-down when Adam finally marries Dinah; it is not much consolation to learn that this happy union was suggested late in the day by G. H. Lewes, and had not been part of the author's original intentions. It is only fair to point out that this was George Eliot's first novel, and that she was still learning how to write.

Whether the characters in the book are sufficiently realistic may also be debated. Perhaps Adam and Dinah are too good to be true, but they are a standing rebuke to those who say that goodness is uninteresting. The author presents them as capable of further improvement, and as examples of the religion of humanity. In the same way that the parishioners of Amos Barton finally rally round their parson, feeling rather 'that the clergyman needed their material aid, than that they needed his spiritual aid', so Dinah and Adam are valued less for their Christianity than for exhibiting that practical and active goodness which reaches out to other people: Adam projects himself into and through his work (Ch. 1 and the little sermon on p. 53), and Dinah, though she impresses us by her preaching, is not above helping Lisbeth. Though both are involved in these human relations at the beginning of the novel, more still is required of them. There is a sense in which both are innocent, and seem to live in an unfallen Eden. Adam is too hard on other people, and must be transformed by sorrow into sympathy; there is a full discussion of the process in Chapter 50 (p. 531). Dinah too must learn, in the end, to substitute a new kind of loving, the particular, for the general benevolence which she has hitherto exercised in the communities of Hayslope and Snowfield; most readers do not understand this, and feel that her marriage is rather a come-down for her.

The two villains, if that is the right word for such human sinners, are Arthur and Hetty. The presentation of Arthur is the great success of the novel, and a passage illustrating it will be examined later. Meanwhile Hetty demands our full attention and compassion. Although she will have to bear, and does bear, the real suffering in the novel, and in anybody else's hands would be a potentially tragic figure, the voice of the author intervenes repeatedly to warn us against her. For example, we are told that she has a 'little silly imagination' (p. 145), that she has a 'little brain' (p. 365) with 'poor narrow thoughts' (p. 415), and even when we are allowed to share her consciousness (Ch. 15, pp. 196–7) it is presented in a demeaning manner; we are not allowed to forget what attitude we are meant to take when the author's voice returns with the words 'little puss' in the middle of page 197. Whereas all the other characters have somebody to relate to—for example, Mr Irwine looks after his sickly sister, and Mrs Poyser seems besotted with Totty—and can therefore obtain their Feuerbachian redemption through sympathy with others, Hetty is described as one of the 'young souls' who are 'as unsympathetic as butterflies sipping nectar; they are isolated from all appeals by a barrier of dreams' (p. 146). Even her genuine efforts to help are spurned (Ch. 14, pp. 191–3); when the author does relent, for example on pages 408–9 where Hetty manages the household very creditably while Mrs Poyser is lying upstairs, this is described by Mr Poyser as an attempt to impress Adam with her housekeeping. Yet it must be said that 'The Journey in Despair' is one of the most moving chapters in the book, approaching the peculiar intensity of the poet Crabbe in its 'dull misery'; and Hetty is finally allowed, on the morning of her execution and after being 'saved' by Dinah, to redeem herself by her voluntary offering of love to Adam in *his* sorrow (p. 506). Nevertheless, even if she is allowed this moment of salvation, the total impression of Hetty in the novel is surely rather odd for an author who is supposed, as a realist, to be able to contemplate the most unattractive examples of humanity and extend sympathy to all.

Though *Adam Bede* is presented to us by the author as a realistic fiction, there are none of the 'life-like' meanderings of the story of 'Amos Barton'. The book is a finished example of the novelist's art; in fact it seems almost too clever if we turn it over and look at the works beneath the clockface of the surface narrative. For example, Hetty is consistently associated with the 'woods' in which her love begins (Ch. 12 and 13), and in which her baby dies. In Chapter 15, 'The Two Bedchambers', Dinah rises to an intuitive level of perception about her companion:

> this feeling about Hetty had gathered a painful intensity; her imagination had created a thorny thicket of sin and sorrow, in which she saw the poor thing struggling torn and bleeding, looking with tears for rescue and finding none.
>
> p. 203

At the end of the same chapter Hetty's dreams take her back into the wood. On page 410 the scene of the baby's death is anticipated: 'if you came close to one spot behind a small bush' you would hear 'a despairing human sob'. These references build to Hetty's confession:

> I did do it, Dinah. . . . I buried it in the wood . . . the little baby . . . and it cried.
>
> p. 497

and

Hetty Sorrel, *steel-engraving after Jozef Israels. From a Dutch translation of* Adam Bede, *1870. An example of a contemporary illustration*

HETTY SORREL

Sacred and Profane Love by Titian. (The title is late. It is now thought that Divine Love is shown naked and Natural Love is clothed). An example of a contrasted 'double picture' which George Eliot imitates in her presentation of Hetty and Dinah in 'The Two Bedchambers', see Adam Bede Chapter 15

> Dinah, do you think God will take away that crying and the place in the wood, now I've told everything?
>
> p. 500

Much more could be unravelled in this way. The patterning in the structure of the novel is evident from the table of contents: the chapters often have matching titles, such as 'The Journey in Hope' and 'The Journey in Despair'. Most things come in twos, and the relations between the characters illustrate this. 'The Two Bedchambers' is once again the best example: Hetty looks into the mirror while Dinah looks *out* into the world (p. 202). This chapter is so carefully worked out, yet so psychologically convincing, that Dinah and Hetty have been compared to two *halves* of one personality; I doubt whether pursuing this direction will help us to understand the novel, though it may help us to analyse its creator. It is more important to see that Hetty's final *rejection* of Dinah's sympathy at the end of the chapter (p. 206) is never 'paired off' until the confession of Hetty to Dinah in the prison; on page 494 we are reminded of the earlier occasion.

Similar pairings exist between Arthur and Adam: there are two occasions of confession to Mr Irwine in Chapters 16 and 39. A link is made on page 453: 'It was a bitter remembrance to him now—that morning when Arthur breakfasted with him, and seemed as if he were on the verge of a confession.' Although the two fight in the wood in Chapter 27, the reconciliation also takes place in the wood in Chapter 48. It may be that the original stimulus for these matching scenes comes from painting.

Although in *Adam Bede* the ideals of the realist programme were certainly modified, its 'truth' impressed the reading public. It became a best-seller, and established George Eliot as a novelist. Queen Victoria informed the Princess Royal that

> Dear Papa is much amused and interested by Adam Bede, which I am delighted to read a second time. There is such knowledge of human nature, and such truth in the characters, I like to trace a likeness to the dear Highlanders in Adam. . . .

The principal delight of the Queen, as of many other readers, was the sayings of Mrs Poyser, 'one of those untaught wits that help to stock a country with proverbs' (p. 397). In saying this, Mr Irwine reminds us once again of von Riehl and the peasantry. Mrs Poyser says of Mr Craig, for example, that she had

> nothing to say again' him, on'y it was a pity he couldna be hatched o'er again, an' hatched different.

It was this common touch which made George Eliot 'a popular as well as a great author', as John Blackwood informed her. She herself had no mock-modesty about the book, and wrote in her journal on 30 November 1858: 'I love it very much and am deeply grateful to have written it.'

Prose extract: . . . a sort of backstairs influence . . .

'. . . But I never knew you so inclined for moral discussion, Arthur? Is it some danger of your own that you are considering in this philosophical, general way?'

In asking this question, Mr Irwine pushed his plate away, threw himself back in his chair, and looked straight at Arthur. He really suspected that Arthur wanted to tell him something, and thought of smoothing the way for him by this direct question. But he was mistaken. Brought suddenly and involuntarily to the brink of confession, Arthur shrank back, and felt less disposed towards it than ever. The conversation had taken a more serious tone than he had intended—it would quite mislead Irwine—he would imagine there was a deep passion for Hetty, while there was no such thing. He was conscious of colouring, and was annoyed at his boyishness.

'O no, no danger,' he said, as indifferently as he could, 'I don't know that I am more liable to irresolution than other people; only there are little incidents now and then that set one speculating on what might happen in the future.'

Was there a motive at work under this strange reluctance of Arthur's which had a sort of backstairs influence, not admitted to himself? Our mental business is carried on much in the same way as the business of the State: a great deal of hard work is done by agents who are not acknowledged. In a piece of machinery, too, I believe there is often a small unnoticeable wheel which has a great deal to do with the motion of the large obvious ones. Possibly, there was some such unrecognised agent secretly busy in Arthur's mind at this moment—possibly it was the fear lest he might hereafter find the fact of having made a confession to the Rector a serious annoyance, in case he should *not* be able quite to carry out his good resolutions? I dare not assert that it was not so. The human soul is a very complex thing.

Adam Bede, Ch. 16, p. 218

CONTEXT Arthur has made up his mind to tell Mr Irwine about his affair with Hetty. After a long preliminary chat over *breakfast*— a nice Victorian period touch which may not have been the fashion of the 1790s—Arthur hesitates, and wonders what to do. Mr Irwine now tries to lead him to a moment of confession, but to no avail.

POINT OF VIEW In modern novels it is usually the custom to adhere to one point of view; this may be the 'over-view' of the author, but it is more common to narrate the story from the point of view of one character. George Eliot used to be regarded as rather old-fashioned, or even as incompetent, because she switches the point of view many times, sometimes even within a paragraph. With the growth of recent theories of fiction, more attention is paid to the way in which George Eliot is able to use all the weapons at the novelist's disposal, and she is praised for switching from the author's voice (the 'narrator') into the speech ('drama') and the thoughts of her characters ('concealed indirect speech').

In the passage we begin with direct speech from Mr Irwine, then the author describes his actions, and then his thoughts—'He really suspected that....' The author's voice comes again—'But ... mistaken.' In the next sentence there is a slide from the author's voice to Arthur's point of view; the words 'felt less disposed' are really concealed indirect speech—'felt that he was less disposed'—and this is the syntactical value of the next sentence: 'The conversation ...' etc., which must mean 'He said to himself that the conversation had....' The repeated 'would ... would ...' serves to continue his thoughts, which come back into the world of 'fact' with 'was ... was ... was ...'. We are then given his actual words to Irwine; in a dramatised version of the novel I suppose that all the preceding paragraph would be omitted, yet it is there that the 'drama' has taken place.

Arthur has, in a sense, *lied* to Irwine—not of course a word to use about oneself; but he has concealed the truth, and the author meditates upon this. She probes relentlessly into his motives, but pretends not to understand them; this is a paradox, because Arthur is her creation, isn't he? George Eliot is often said to 'moralise', but is that the right word here? She begins by asking questions, speculates about the inside of the mind, then of Arthur's mind; but she does not 'tell' us; she runs away, it seems, from the direct account— 'I dare not assert that it was not so.'

This is a very strange point of view indeed; yet most people, asked to give an account of the paragraph, would, I think, say that the author *does* 'tell' us a lot about Arthur, and George Eliot is praised for her 'psychological realism'. This can only mean, and we approach a very difficult area here, that we translate the negative 'ironies' in the passage—and there are many—into positive 'statements' in giving an account of it. And so the final sentence is quite a problem; *either* it is straight— 'I do not understand the human mind'—*or* it is ironical— 'In spite of all his gentlemanly surface, Arthur is a simple soul, and a bad one at that. Dear reader, you have a lot to learn.'

It is the fascination of reading George Eliot that neither of these opposed readings of the text will really satisfy; the text remains, in a sense, 'potential', leaving the individual reader to make of it what he or she can.

ARTHUR'S PRESENTATION IN THE NOVEL The character of Arthur is one of the great successes of George Eliot's fiction. This short passage is insufficient evidence, and it is worth looking at the whole of Chapters 12 and 13, in particular at the counter-movements in his mind described on pages 173 and 178–9. D. H. Lawrence saw this as a major advance in the technique available to the novelist:

> You see, it was really George Eliot who started it all. . . . It was she who started putting all the action inside. Before, you know, with Fielding and the others, it had been outside.
> Jessie Chambers, *D. H. Lawrence, A Personal Record*

8 Contrasting heroines: Maggie and Romola

Maggie Tulliver has a particular place in the history of Feminism. For example, in *The Second Sex* Simone de Beauvoir repeatedly refers to 'Maggie in *The Mill on the Floss*, in whom George Eliot embodied the doubts and brave rebellions of her youth against Victorian England'. Brave words indeed, but whether this is really what the book is about is a difficult question. We are told that Maggie 'rebelled against her lot' (p. 380), and this 'lot', as we shall see in the second paragraph of the passage on 'A variation of Protestantism . . .', is the misfortune of being born into the wrong family and into a narrow and unfeeling society. Because she is also born into the wrong sex, she does not get the opportunities offered to Tom, though here is must be said that the novel is ambiguous: Tom's 'lot' is equally restricted, and his superior education is seen to have no real value. Maggie is desperate for education, and succumbs to a variety of books; it is worth noting that the books are also known to have been loved by Mary Ann Evans, though Maggie discovers them at an earlier age. Thomas à Kempis is particularly interesting: a medieval Christian writer, who believed that renouncing the world was not a negative but a positive act, because it would lead to a mystical inner life and ultimately to union with Christ in the Sacrament of Communion. In *The Mill on the Floss*, the message of his book is made one of 'resignation'; we must renounce and endure (Bk IV, Ch. 3, pp. 382-5).

Though this great teacher tells Maggie to submit, it is a long time before she accepts that this is her duty; it is not that she cannot take good advice, but she is incapable of relating to the situation in which she finds herself. For Maggie is a Romantic in the great tradition. In the same way that Wordsworth, in *The Prelude*, announced that 'I was not for that time, nor for that place,' so too the young Mary Ann Evans remembered that:

> When I was quite a little child I could not be satisfied with the things around me.
>
> *Letters*, I 22

Maggie knows that in some other place, or time, she would be in the right:

> In books there were people who were always agreeable or tender . . . who did not show their kindness by finding fault . . . Maggie

was a creature full of eager passionate longings for all that was beautiful and glad: thirsty for all knowledge: with an ear straining after dreamy music that died away and would not come near to her: with a blind, unconscious yearning for something that would link together the wonderful impressions of this mysterious life and give her soul a sense of home in it.

pp. 319–20

At times the situation becomes paranoiac. The Dodsons, who consider themselves to be normal people, regard Maggie as abnormal; to us, the readers, on the other hand, she seems to be a normal person living in an abnormal society. She is one of the 'new people', whom we shall meet again in George Eliot's later novels: she is a 'modern' consciousness trapped in an early-nineteenth-century bottle, from which she can't get out, though we, author and readers, know that she is in the right and that the other people in the book are wrong. The situation is so vivid that we are pulled down into her world: she, on the other hand, is so vital a character that she transcends it, and lives beyond the book in her potentiality—we could make up a future for her in the modern world as we could for Dorothea at the end of *Middlemarch*.

Faced with this insoluble problem, it seems hardly fair to complain that Maggie's aspirations do not seem specific enough to lead anywhere: 'she often strove after too high a flight and came down with her poor little half-fledged wings dabbled in the mud' (p. 386). In fact, she does earn her living as a teacher, but those years of her life are hardly referred to in the text (pp. 481–2). Nor is it very easy to see, on the strictly logical level, why she should deserve such a terrible death; in spite of the determinism which seems to underlie the novel—'our life is determined for us' (p.397)—a shift of emphasis takes place towards the end. There is a revealing discussion on page 514 of the book, in which we are informed that you cannot prophesy what is going to happen from character alone; indeed character is 'not the whole of our destiny'. And so the climax of Maggie's fortune is the result of chance events; Stephen Guest rows her down the river instead of the expected Philip Wakem (pp. 587–8), and the death-dealing flood, which in the real world might be called an act of God, seems to be a capricious intervention by the author.

The Mill on the Floss, then, begins as a comedy, changes into a family saga, and and ends as an unexpected 'tragedy'. Although the story is told in the third person, the reader is led to identify with Maggie; the conflicts aroused in Maggie, and therefore in the mind of the reader, cannot, at any rate at first reading, be seen from a balanced point of view; certainly in the second half of the book these conflicts are not distanced or filtered by the usual stratagems of fiction, so that one seems to have been reading private letters or, in the extreme moments of anguish, having one's own privacy violated. The usual explanation given for this is that the writer is guilty of using autobiographical material; that there are parallels to the life of Marian Evans cannot be denied, but it does not follow that the use of autobiography must lead to a bad or uncontrolled work of fiction. Indeed, the doctrine of realism might well have led George Eliot to decide that her own life would make a better basis for a novel than her observations of other people.

It is the parallel between the children in the novel and Mary Ann and Isaac Evans which is worth exploring in order to resolve why the novel becomes so intense, and ends in such a strange way. Tom and Maggie are born in the same years as the Evans children, and their cousin Lucy is presumably Chrissey, the tidy Evans sibling. In the pre-adolescent years the brother-sister relationship is identified with the state of innocence; it may be debated how far Tom really 'wandered hand-in-hand' with Maggie, but when she grows up she 'remembers' this to have been so. Her attempts to relate to other males are dogged by Tom with unfeeling prohibitions. For her 'sexual misconduct' she is punished by being driven away, and only in death can the true relationship with Tom be resumed. To go outside the novel for a moment, the scene on page 612, where Maggie is rejected by her brother for 'going down the river' with Stephen, is surely related to Marian's rejection by Isaac in 1857 after her sexual misdemeanour with Lewes had become known: indeed, that liaison had had its public commencement in a departure by boat for the Continent. Tom appeals to the patriarchal sky-god: 'You have disgraced my father's name,' and is answered with storm and rain. These rather primitive readings of the text may seem uncalled-for, but I bring them into the discussion to show why there is a logic which unites the conclusion of the novel to the whole story, at any rate in the mind of the author. The guilt, which Marian Evans could not feel on an intellectual level as a disciple of Feuerbach, leaks out in the emotional pattern of the novel. The ending of the book is wishful thinking, a carrying over of the remorse which she was unable to suppress any longer.

Although the book is not the autonomous fiction which it might have been, it is worth considering how and why such a long and intense novel as this ever gets written. The drive to cleanse the mind of obsessive personal problems may not seem the best way to account for works of art, but is is certainly one of the motives for literary creation. Having freed oneself from the obsession, two courses are possible; either to stop writing, because the motive has disappeared, or to load onself with an intellectual task as a substitute for the emotional driving force. This is one explanation of the total change of direction which George Eliot's next novel represents. The problems which Maggie had to face—the loneliness of the newly fledged modern personality, the need of an educated woman for worthwhile *action* in her life—will return in *Middlemarch* to confront Dorothea; meanwhile, in *Romola*, she will consider how a different kind of woman might have come to terms with the society of Florence at the end of the Middle Ages.

Unlike George Eliot's other novels, *Romola* is set in a remote past; the only works we could put alongside it are poems, such as *The Spanish Gypsy*. Historical novels were popular, because of the example of Sir Walter Scott, whose works were often set in the medieval past; Robert Evans had loved Scott, and Mary Ann had had to read his novels to her father in the 1840s. Historical novels were also considered to be worthwhile exercises for the human mind; the attempt to understand previous stages of human society by writing imaginative works was acceptable to the Victorians—we might compare the high status given to historical painting. Purists who feel that this is not 'history' may take some comfort from the fact that G. H. Lewes called *Romola* a 'Romance'.

As the story is unlikely to be familiar to the twentieth-century reader, some account of it is necessary. After a sweeping visionary Proem, reminding us that 'we still resemble the men of the past more than we differ from them', we are set down in fifteenth-century Florence; the year is actually 1492. Tito Melema, a young and attractive Greek of uncertain origins, is discovered asleep in a back-street of Florence. After a number of rather tedious chapters, which serve to provide the necessary local colour of Florentine life, he is introduced to Romola, the high-born daughter of a blind scholar. Tito is only interested in improving his fortunes; marriage to Romola will be necessary as part of his career. Meanwhile he is in love with Tessa, probably one of the dimmest girls in fiction; after his marriage to Romola takes place, he will continue to see Tessa, by whom he has two children.

At first, then, the psychological interest of the novel is within Tito's consciousness rather than Romola's; he is a man who has always 'tried to slip away from everything unpleasant'—for example, he was supposed to ransom his former protector, his 'father' Baldassarre. Having arrived safely himself in Florence, he forgets this inconvenient reminder of his past, and assumes that Baldassarre is dead; in fact, Baldassarre returns, is disowned by Tito, and so becomes his enemy; he will pursue the young man like Nemesis.

Meanwhile Romola, brought up by her father to despise Christianity and to adopt Renaissance 'paganism', has come under the influence of Savonarola. He is, of course, a real historical personage, and George Eliot is concerned to incorporate a considerable amount of information about him in her story; we are shown how his preaching affected the Florentines, and how he taught them to 'burn their vanities' and repent before Florence was destroyed by God. Political events appear to confirm his prophecies, and his personal magnetism is demonstrated by his conversion of Romola, who was about to desert her feckless husband. Instead she learns to accept her lot and we become, through her activities, involved in the miseries of the Florentines during these years. The novel ends strangely; Tito is murdered by Baldassarre, but Romola drifts away from the Tuscan coast in an empty boat, and arrives in a village stricken by plague. She performs sensible 'Florence Nightingale' actions, and is believed by the villagers to be the Madonna. (This episode, in Chapters 68–9, was the original 'germ' of the story, and is worth looking up as an example of Victorian fantasy about the Middle Ages.) This dream-like excursion gives her new strength of character, and she returns to Florence. There she discovers and adopts Tessa and her children. Savonarola is burnt in 1498, but an epilogue set in 1509 shows Romola firmly in control of her new household.

Setting Romola's story in the period of Savonarola leads to several kinds of difficulty for the novelist. Savonarola was a typical nineteenth-century subject for rehabilitation; though he might be regarded as a religious fanatic and a dictator, he could also be seen as representing liberal tendencies and the forward movement of history. We could compare the way in which Carlyle's *Letters and Speeches of Oliver Cromwell* changed Victorian opinion about that period of our history. In discussing Savonarola's preaching, George Eliot observes:

> Perhaps, while no preacher ever had a more massive influence than Savonarola, no preacher ever had more heterogeneous materials to work upon. And one secret of the massive influence lay in the highly mixed character of his preaching. Baldassarre, wrought into an ecstasy of self-martyring revenge, was only an extreme case among the partial and narrow sympathies of that audience. In Savonarola's preaching there were strains that appealed to the very finest susceptibilities of men's natures, and there were elements that gratified low egoism, tickled gossiping curiosity, and fascinated timorous superstition. His need of personal predominance, his labyrinthine allegorical interpretations of the Scriptures, his enigmatic visions, and his false certitude about the Divine intentions, never ceased, in his own large soul, to be ennobled by that fervid piety, that passionate sense of the infinite, that active sympathy, that clear-sighted demand for the subjection of selfish interests to the general good, which he had in common with the greatest of mankind. . . .

The Burning of the Vanities *by Mrs Jane Benham Hay.* See Romola *Chapter 49—'The Pyramid of Vanities'*

The scene is the main square of Florence, in front of the Baptistery, whose bronze doors can be seen in the centre of the picture. The procession of youths in white robes, olive wreaths and red crosses, are seen collecting the vanities together. Notice from left to right:—

three gamblers, about to hand over their dice.
the large lady, surrendering "a reddened ball" of rouge to the first youth
the lady to her right, giving her jewels to the second youth
the deacon, carrying books to be burnt
the youths in the centre have collected carpets, tapestries and works of art.

One is treading a peacock's feather underfoot.
the Dominican is carrying the banner together with an artist—notice the palette at his belt with a little red cross above it: he may be Lorenzo Credi or even Botticelli, who became a Piagnone.
the musicians are presumably to be taken positively, i.e. the instruments are not for burning. The girl looking towards us may be "an angel", in that she is picked out as having an excessively white face and a blue dress painted with the words Gloria in Excelsis Deo
finally there are four Florentine worthies, who have also taken the emblem of the red cross.

The picture is approximately 2 metres × 5 metres, and hangs in the hall of Homerton College, Cambridge.

> It was the fashion of old, when an ox was led out for sacrifice to Jupiter, to chalk the dark spots, and give the offering a false show of unblemished whiteness. Let us fling away the chalk, and boldly say,—the victim is spotted, but it is not therefore in vain that his mighty heart is laid on the altar of men's highest hopes.
>
> Ch. 25, pp. 299–300

This is the voice of the historian regarding events from outside rather than the novelist working from within a character, and it has always been felt that the portrayal of Savonarola is less than satisfactory; in particular, the climaxes of his career, the Trial by Fire, and his death by burning, are muffled and uncertainly described, as if George Eliot felt the need to withdraw herself from the situation. It must be observed that though he can simply be considered as a good 'Evangelical preacher' who had the misfortune to live before the Reformation, this is not why he was important to the Florentines in his own day; his strange prophecies and his reputation as a worker of miracles were what made him famous. These aspects of his career are unacceptable to Positivist thinking, so that George Eliot stresses the practical side of Savonarola's teaching. In the novel, the rich give up their vanities to provide silver to alleviate suffering; after Romola's conversion she works among the poor during the famine—that is to say, she practises a medieval version of the religion of humanity. Romola is always reluctant to give credence to the supernatural aspects of Christianity: she is too much of a nineteenth-century intellectual for that.

> No radiant angel came across the gloom with a clear message for her. In those times, as now, there were human beings who never saw angels or heard perfectly clear messages. Such truth as came to them was brought confusedly in the voices and deeds of men not at all like the seraphs of unfailing wing and piercing vision— men who believed falsities as well as truths, and did the wrong as well as the right. The helping hands stretched out to them were the hands of men who stumbled and often saw dimly, so that these beings unvisited by angels had no other choice than to grasp that stumbling guidance along the path of reliance and action which is the path of life, or else to pause in loneliness and disbelief, which is no path, but the arrest of inaction and death.
>
> Ch. 36, p. 396

Yet because the novel is set in the past rather than in Victorian England, with a modern Romola helping in a cholera epidemic, for example, George Eliot is able to exploit some hidden advantages.

The Visible Madonna *by Sir Frederic Leighton, illustrating* Romola *Chapter 44*

We can contemplate the situation of a man with two wives, a stupid one with children and an intelligent one without any, and ignore the parallels which might otherwise come to mind. G. H. Lewes, Agnes Lewes and Marian Evans do not intrude themselves upon our consideration; there is no feeling of hypocrisy, rather a refreshing candour and even a kind of humour about the extra-marital escapades.

George Eliot also places Romola in situations which anticipate those of the heroines of *Felix Holt* and *Middlemarch*. In the first place, Romola, like Dorothea and Esther, is the young girl who helps an old scholar; Romola's father is blind, and so relies upon her entirely. He cannot finish his book—'that great work in which I had desired to gather, as into a firm web, all the threads that my research had laboriously disentangled . . .' (p. 97). He leaves her his library, which becomes a problem to dispose of according to his dying wish; this again is a situation which foretells that of Dorothea after the death of Casaubon. In order to find help, she turns to a younger man. Tito is perniciously attractive, and flits about like a Renaissance version of Will Ladislaw.

Romola also looks forward to *Felix Holt* and *Middlemarch* because the personal stories are blended with an attempt to study society at a crucial turning-point. Romola is seen to grow by becoming involved in the political events. At first she is not interested at all:

> To Romola these grave political changes had gathered their chief interest from their bearing on the fulfilment of her father's wish. She had been brought up in learned seclusion from the interests of actual life, and had been accustomed to think of heroic deeds and great principles as something antithetic to the vulgar present, of the Pnyx and the Forum as something more worthy of attention than the councils of living Florentine men. And now the expulsion of the Medici meant little more for her than the extinction of her best hope about her father's library. The times, she knew, were unpleasant for friends of the Medici, like her godfather and Tito: superstitious shopkeepers and the stupid rabble were full of suspicions; but her new keen interest in public events, in the outbreak of war, in the issue of the French king's visit, in the changes that were likely to happen in the State, was kindled solely by the sense of love and duty to her father's memory. All Romola's ardour had been concentrated in her affections. Her share in her father's learned pursuits had been for her little more than a toil which was borne for his sake; and Tito's airy brilliant faculty had no attraction for her that was not merged in the deeper sympathies that belong to young love and trust. Romola had had contact with no mind that could stir the larger possibilities of her nature; they lay folded and crushed like

embryonic wings, making no element in her consciousness beyond an occasional vague uneasiness.

Ch. 27, p. 311

It is Savonarola who brings the macrocosm of Florence and the microcosm of Romola's soul together; in order to overcome the disappointment of her marriage she learns to embrace the common lot, and to stand up and be counted:

> And the inspiring consciousness breathed into her by Savonarola's influence that her lot was vitally united with the general lot had exalted even the minor details of obligation into religion. She was marching with a great army; she was feeling the stress of a common life. If victims were needed, and it was uncertain on whom the lot might fall, she would stand ready to answer to her name. She had stood long; she had striven hard to fulfil the bond, but she had seen all the conditions which made the fulfilment possible gradually forsaking her. The one effect of her marriage-tie seemed to be the stifling predominance over her of a nature that she despised. All her efforts at union had only made its impossibility more palpable, and the relation had become for her simply a degrading servitude. The law was sacred. Yes, but rebellion might be sacred too. It flashed upon her mind that the problem before her was essentially the same as that which had lain before Savonarola—the problem where the sacredness of obedience ended, and where the sacredness of rebellion began. To her, as to him, there had come one of those moments in life when the soul must dare to act on its own warrant, not only without external law to appeal to, but in the face of a law which is not unarmed with Divine lightnings—lightnings that may yet fall if the warrant has been false.

Ch. 56, pp. 552–3

It is in this identification with the 'great army' that she succeeds; she learns what can be done and what she is capable of performing. Romola's social commitment helps us to understand what Dorothea might have done with her life at a more generous period of history than the nineteenth century.

Although the doctrine of necessity is stressed, and events follow inevitably from the faults in predetermined characters like Tito, the story does end happily. Unlike *The Mill on the Floss*, the novel teaches us that personal grief and misfortune can be overcome; the heroine wins through, and the new generation are seen to inherit the earth. The book is successful both as a Positivist statement and as a portrayal of a new woman, and is important as a counterbalance to the rather melancholy view of George Eliot which readers sometimes abstract from her more famous stories.

Prose extract: A variation of Protestantism . . .

Perhaps something akin to this oppressive feeling may have weighed upon you in watching this old-fashioned family life on the banks of the Floss, which even sorrow hardly suffices to lift above the level of the tragi-comic. It is a sordid life, you say, this of the Tullivers and Dodsons—irradiated by no sublime principles, no romantic visions, no active, self-renouncing faith—moved by none of those wild, uncontrollable passions which create the dark shadows of misery and crime—without that primitive rough simplicity of wants, that hard submissive ill-paid toil, that child-like spelling-out of what nature has written, which gives its poetry to peasant life. Here, one has conventional worldly notions and habits without instruction and without polish—surely the most prosaic form of human life: proud respectability in a gig of unfashionable build: worldliness without side-dishes. Observing these people narrowly, even when the iron hand of misfortune has shaken them from their unquestioning hold on the world, one sees little trace of religion, still less of a distinctively Christian creed. Their belief in the unseen, so far as it manifests itself at all, seems to be rather of a pagan kind: their moral notions, though held with strong tenacity, seem to have no standard beyond hereditary custom. You could not live among such people; you are stifled for want of an outlet towards something beautiful, great, or noble: you are irritated with these dull men and women, as a kind of population out of keeping with the earth on which they live—with this rich plain where the great river flows for ever onward and links the small pulse of the old English town with the beatings of the world's mighty heart. A vigorous superstition that lashes its gods or lashes its own back, seems to be more congruous with the mystery of the human lot, than the mental condition of these emmet-like Dodsons and Tullivers.

I share with you this sense of oppressive narrowness; but it is necessary that we should feel it, if we care to understand how it acted on the lives of Tom and Maggie—how it has acted on young natures in many generations, that in the onward tendency of human things have risen above the mental level of the generation before them, to which they have been nevertheless tied by the strongest fibres of their hearts. The suffering, whether of martyr or victim, which belongs to every historical advance of mankind, is represented in this way in every town and by hundreds of obscure hearths: and we need not shrink from this comparison of small things with great; for does not science tell us that its highest striving is after the ascertainment of a unity which shall bind the smallest things with the greatest? In natural science, I have understood, there is nothing petty to the mind that has a large vision of relations, and to which every single object suggests a vast sum of conditions. It is surely the same with the observation of human life.

Certainly, the religious and moral ideas of the Dodsons and Tullivers were of too specific a kind to be arrived at deductively, from the statement that they were part of the Protestant population of Great Britain. Their theory of life had its core of soundness, as all theories must have on which decent and prosperous families have been reared and have flourished; but it had the very slightest tincture of theology. If, in the maiden days of the Dodson sisters, their bibles opened more easily at some parts than others, it was because of dried tulip petals, which had been distributed quite impartially, without preference for the historical, devotional, or doctrinal. Their religion was of a simple, semi-pagan kind, but there was no heresy in it, if heresy properly means choice, for they didn't know there was any other religion, except that of chapel-goers, which appeared to run in families, like asthma. How *should* they know? The vicar of their pleasant rural parish was not a controversialist, but a good hand at whist, and one who had a joke always ready for a blooming female parishioner. The religion of the Dodsons consisted in revering whatever was customary and respectable: it was necessary to be baptised, else one could not be buried in the churchyard, and to take the sacrament before death as a security against more dimly understood perils; but it was of equal necessity to have the proper pall-bearers and well-cured hams at one's funeral, and to leave an unimpeachable will. A Dodson would not be taxed with the omission of anything that was becoming, or that belonged to that eternal fitness of things which was plainly indicated in the practice of the most substantial parishioners, and in the family traditions—such as obedience to parents, faithfulness to kindred, industry, rigid honesty, thrift, the thorough scouring of wooden and copper utensils, the hoarding of coins likely to disappear from the currency, the production of first-rate commodities for the market, and general preference for whatever was home-made. The Dodsons were a very proud race, and their pride lay in the utter frustration of all desire to tax them with a breach of traditional duty or propriety. A wholesome pride in many respects; since it identified honour with perfect integrity, thoroughness of work, and faithfulness to admitted rules; and society owes some worthy qualities in many of her members to mothers of the Dodson class, who made their butter and their fromenty well and would have felt disgraced to make it otherwise. To be honest and poor was never a Dodson motto, still less, to seem rich though being poor; rather, the family badge was to be honest and rich, and not only rich, but richer than was supposed. To live respected and have the proper bearers at your funeral was an achievement of the ends of existence that would be entirely nullified if on the reading of your Will, you sank in the opinion of your fellow-men either by turning out to be poorer than they expected or by leaving your money in a capricious manner without strict regard to degrees of kin. The right thing must always be done towards kindred: the right thing was to correct them severely, if they were other than a credit to the family, but still not to alienate from them the smallest rightful share in the family shoe-buckles and other property. A conspicuous quality in the Dodson character was its genuineness: its vices and virtues alike were phases of a proud, honest egoism which had a hearty dislike to whatever made against its own credit and interest, and would be frankly hard of speech to inconvenient 'kin' but would never forsake or ignore them—would not let them want bread, but only require them to eat it with bitter herbs.

The Mill on the Floss, Bk IV, Ch. 1, pp. 362–5

CONTEXT The passage is taken from the middle of a chapter halfway through the novel. Book III had ended with Mr Tulliver, now a broken man, instructing Tom to write his hatred of Lawyer Wakem in the family Bible. This leads to a consideration of the 'paganism' implicit in this action in the first chapter of Book IV, which is called 'A variation of Protestantism unknown to Bossuet', the reference being to the seventeenth-century historian of religion.

SUBJECT MATTER As opposed to the minute attention paid to the inner drama of Arthur's conscience, the emphasis here is on the way in which morality is ultimately a product of geographical and social conditions. In the paragraph preceding our extract the author took an over-view of human life, which was considered to be in the most part 'a narrow ugly grovelling existence'. We then move to the position of a sociologist or anthropologist, and observe the Dodsons and Tullivers as if they were an obscure tribe; one thinks back immediately to von Riehl and his work on the German peasantry.

In the first paragraph it is made clear that the Dodsons are not romantic; nor are they peasants. The humour of 'worldliness without side-dishes' does not really help us to understand them; they are distant from us. The reference to their 'paganism' is similarly off-putting; they are so different from us that 'you', the gentle reader, could not possibly 'live among such people'. Finally, they are dismissed as 'emmet-' or ant-like; we might be observing a non-human life-form, and making notes for a scientific account of it.

In the second paragraph we are prevented from taking all this as just another ironical 'joke', because we are reminded of the real suffering which this limiting existence has brought to Tom and Maggie; the remainder of the book will illustrate this even more conclusively. The main point of the paragraph is, however, more hopeful, and was considered in some detail when we looked at the character of Maggie. There is progress, there is 'advance', there is an 'onward tendency', but unlike the kind of Progress which 'Victorian thinkers' like Herbert Spencer were describing. Every advance is accompanied by human suffering, and 'obscure' people like Maggie are as important as the famous 'martyr or victim'. Everything is of interest to a scientific enquirer; and so we should not feel alienated from the Dodsons but try to understand them.

The third paragraph is one of the best pieces of George Eliot's writing; its analysis of what one must really call 'English' rather than 'Dodson' patterns of behaviour is accurate and amusing at the same time. Their Protestant heritage has become an empty religion of respectability, against which we can contrast Maggie's reading of Thomas à Kempis. The family traditions are not so negative; there is honour here, as well as integrity; the syntactical arrangement of the clauses and sentences builds towards 'richer than was supposed,' which is both the rhythm of a joke on the part of the author and a triumph of the Dodson morality. The importance of wills links back to what we have already observed of the Pearsons (p. 16). Finally, the praise of the 'genuineness' of the Dodsons looks across to Tom's industry, and the reference to not forsaking kin anticipates Maggie's downfall and the surprising intervention of Aunt Glegg; she will offer to take Maggie into her own house (p. 629 ff.).

LOOKING BACKWARD AND FORWARD The Dodsons could be the Poysers; the pastoral glow has disappeared, yet we may be seeing the same people from a more distant viewpoint. Imagine Tottie grown up into Maggie, and become critical of her parents; or, alternatively, consider Maggie's 'sin' as a milder version of Hetty's crime—the loneliness of both girls before the unrelenting hounding of them by their own society. Dr Leavis projects the Dodsons forward as well, and sees them reappear in *Middlemarch*, 'the tribe that foregathers at Stone Court waiting for Peter Featherstone to die'.

Interior of St Michael's Church, Coventry by David Gee, 1862. A scene from provincial life.

9 *Felix Holt* and *Middlemarch* as political novels

After the foreign settings of *Romola* and *The Spanish Gypsy*—a dramatic poem which she struggled with until finally G. H. Lewes took it away from her—George Eliot returned in *Felix Holt* to her own country and the time of her youth. The story takes place in North Loamshire, which is presumably North Warwickshire, and the town of Treby Magna is Nuneaton. It was in that town that Mary Anne had witnessed an election riot in 1832, and such a riot will feature in the novel. Although the action is carefully set in the period 1832–3, after the passing of the first Reform Bill, it is also a topical novel, because the period of its composition coincided with the debates about the further extension of the franchise; so that Felix's doubts about this (p. 399 ff.), which seem rather out of place in 1833, are an address to the readers of 1866. The second Reform Bill was finally passed in 1867.

The Author's Introduction, with its wide-ranging description of the scenery of the English Midlands, establishes that the story which will follow is to be about 'the condition of England'. It also reminds us once again of von Riehl and his work on the *natural history* of the peasantry—the human beings are a product of the soil which also nourishes and sustains them: the variations in the underlying geology lead to different occupations among the people, who become agriculturalists, basket-makers, weavers, or bow-legged miners. In turn, these trades lead their practitioners to group themselves into village or town communities, and the manufacturing town, with its 'riots and trades-union meetings', is contrasted with the apparent backwardness and political inertia of the rural region. This magnificent introductory chapter to *Felix Holt* should also be read before embarking upon *Middlemarch*, with its revealing subtitle—'A Study of Provincial Life'.

Felix Holt has a double plot, and the intertwining of two stories can also be seen as a preparation for the complex design of *Middlemarch*. The two stories are linked by the character of Esther Lyon; her crucial rôle in the novel will be discussed in a moment. For many readers the most important woman in the whole book is Mrs Transome; we meet her in the first chapter of the novel, and her presence seems to dominate the book. Mrs Transome is entrapped by actions which she has committed in the past, and her resemblance to the heroines of Greek tragedy is marked (see Chapter 39 in particular); George Eliot has drawn a portrait so full of tragic irony that the novel gains a great deal from a second reading. Although she is a profoundly unhappy woman, she seems to have one potential source of joy in her son Harold. His return from fifteen years' absence in Turkey opens the action of the novel. She has hoped that he will open a route through to the 'future' for her—out of the past into which she is locked. It is obvious, however, from the moment that he begins to speak, that there is not going to be a profound relationship; the two cannot even communicate. The division between them is accentuated by the fact that Mrs Transome, as a member of the established landed gentry and a natural ruler, is a Tory; Harold, on the other hand, is resolved to stand in the coming election as a Radical candidate. This seems to be the only way for the Tory party to retain power, now that it has been overtaken by events. It must take up ground to the 'left' of that occupied by the victorious proponents of Reform: see pages 195–6 for a comical newspaper account of the situation. No profound analysis is really necessary, however, for Harold is simply a political opportunist.

In this he is in stark contrast to Felix Holt, whose varied fortunes are part of the parallel story. Though he describes himself as a Radical, it is rather more difficult to sort out his politics than those of Harold Transome; in fact it would be difficult to imagine Felix as a member of any political party, since he is not prepared to compromise his position at all. He is a man of principle of a very old-fashioned kind, and it is significant that he gets on famously with Rufus Lyon, who represents an older generation of Nonconformist preachers. Felix's radicalism is a moral stand, a rejection of 'getting on in society'. In spite of his exposure to higher education he is resolved to stay a 'working-man'; he is not an agitator, and in his speeches he is more concerned with inculcating 'a change of heart' than inciting revolution. It is not difficult to imagine him eventually becoming a secular preacher; in the same way that Rufus cannot refrain from advising his congregation about politics in his sermons, Felix lectures his audience about morality in his political speeches. It is not surprising that when he suggests that the vote in itself will do little good, he finds himself being cheered by the Tories.

Esther Lyon is the key figure in the extremely complicated plot. After her parentage is discovered she is revealed to be the true heir to the Transome estate, and is placed in a situation where there is a choice between ways of life and marriage-partners. Either she takes the Transome inheritance together with Harold, or she rejects it for a doubtful future with Felix Holt, who at that moment is at the lowest ebb of his fortunes, having been sent to prison on account of his conduct during the election riot. While the dilemma is made believable and human by the author, so that love triumphs over all difficulties, it is not difficult to see an allegory in this story. In a novel about England, Mrs Transome and her kind are representatives of the Tory gentry, determined to maintain the power structure and the social relations of the *past*; Harold's attempt to get into Parliament by pretending to be a Radical does not succeed, since he had no real intention of giving anything away. Felix Holt, whatever we make of his strange politics, is, like Ladislaw in *Middlemarch*, a new kind of emancipated intellectual, and represents the *future*. In choosing Felix, Esther, who is in some sense the conscience of the middle classes and the heir to the estate (England), sees where the country is heading; she rejects the false shams of the gentry and allies herself with the class which will come to power in the future. Though this analysis is extremely crude, it will perhaps become easier to follow when compared with a similar movement of mind in the greater novel—*Middlemarch*.

Both in general design and points of detail *Felix Holt* may be seen as a trial run for George Eliot's next novel. In this section I propose to keep very strictly to the political theme, and to give the background to *Middlemarch* as a table of historical events. The novel is set in the years *before* the first Reform Bill was passed, and therefore antedates the setting of *Felix Holt*.

	EVENTS IN HISTORY	ALLUSIONS IN MIDDLEMARCH
1829	Wellington governs with Peel's support; the Tories remain in power until November 1830	'When George IV was still reigning over the privacies of Windsor, when the Duke of Wellington was Prime Minister . . .' (p. 219).
	(April) Catholic Emancipation Bill passed.	Mr Casaubon, the Rector of Lowick, has written 'a very seasonable pamphlet on the Catholic question' (p. 90) which may lead to a bishopric 'if Peel stays in' (p. 62). (30 September) *Middlemarch* begins. (November) Dorothea Brooke marries Casaubon and goes to Rome.
1830		The Casaubons return 'in the middle of January' (p. 306).

	(3 May) Peel inherits a baronetcy. (26 June) George IV dies. General election (July) Revolution in France	'the celebrated Peel, now Sir Robert' (p. 344). See p. 392 ff. Will Ladislaw is editing the *Pioneer*. 'they're in the next century . . . on the other side of the water' (p. 417).
	(15 September) Huskisson killed by a train. He had wished to reform a number of boroughs, including East Retford. (Autumn) Disturbances among farm labourers, including the breaking of machines. (November) Whigs in power under Grey.	'railway . . . pretty well seasoned now it had done for Huskisson' (p. 452). East Retford notorious for bribery (p. 419).
1831	(March) Reform Bill passes Commons by one vote and soon runs into difficulties. (22 April) Parliament dissolved. General election; there is a swing to Reform.	Casaubon dies. In his will Dorothea is told that she loses her inheritance if she marries Ladislaw. Mr Brooke stands for Parliament as an independent; he is forced to withdraw (Ch. 51).
	(24 June) Reform Bill again introduced. (22 September) Bill passes Commons. (8 October) Bill is thrown out by the House of Lords. Riots in Nottingham, Derby and Bristol. (12 December) Reform Bill is introduced to Commons for third time and carried.	
1832		(March) Lydgate and Bulstrode talk about 'the chances of the Reform Bill in the House of Lords' (p. 765); Lords and Reform again mentioned (p. 774).

(13 April) Reform Bill passes Lords but is blocked in committee. The King is asked to create new peers. (9–14 May) Grey's government resigns. More popular agitation. Tories cannot form a government. King sends for Grey again. (7 June) Reform Bill finally passed and receives Royal Assent.	'It was just after the Lords had thrown out the Reform Bill' (p. 871). 'intended creation of peers' (p. 871) *Middlemarch* ends in May. Dorothea marries Will on or about the same date. In the Finale (p. 894) Will Ladislaw becomes an MP for 'a constituency who paid his expenses'.

George Eliot has often been praised for her historical accuracy, and a number of the allusions have little or no function beyond that of reminding us of the period in which the novel is set. This in itself earns commendations for careful construction, and it must be obvious that the author made use of a calendar; but a merely mechanical exactness of reference is not in itself necessarily desirable in a work of imagination, and critics have long ceased censuring Shakespeare for his anachronisms. There must be some point in the choice of these three years; in *Felix Holt* George Eliot had stated that 'there is no private life which has not been determined by a wider public life' (Ch. 3, p. 129), and it would be reasonable to ask in what way Dorothea's changes of heart are related to the political events.

Without going to an extreme point of view and suggesting that *Middlemarch* is an allegorical novel in which all the characters represent a particular party or tendency, it seems to me that a parallel movement can be detected to that in *Felix Holt*, and that Dorothea's choices are similar to those made by Esther Lyon. For instance, Dorothea's marriages, first to a Tory who sides with Peel and secondly to a young Liberal Reformer, run alongside the political crisis and its resolution: George Eliot must have intended that the intelligent reader should spot that the marriage to Will takes place on virtually the same day as the Reform Bill is passed. The storm of Chapter 83, where Will and Dorothea hold hands against the fury of the elements, is open to another interpretation than the storm of passion which mere reasoning intelligences cannot control, and can be seen to represent the storm of resentment and popular fury which is engulfing England at the frustration of Reform and the onward tendency of historical determinism.

This leads to a reading of the entire novel in which the historical background is not merely 'wallpaper'. Dorothea, brought up among the landed gentry who represent the Old Order, whether they are Whig (Brooke) or Tory (Chettam and Casaubon), finds out that they are in their various ways ineffective as guardians, husbands or political figures (Brooke cannot manage his estate, Chettam and Casaubon are not really interested in building cottages for their people). In this pattern of ideas the passage at the foot of p. 846 becomes meaningful:

> And what sort of crisis might not this be in three lives whose contact with hers laid an obligation on her as if they had been suppliants bearing the sacred branch? The objects of her rescue were not to be sought out by her fancy: they were chosen for her. She yearned towards the perfect Right, that it might make a throne within her, and rule her errant will. 'What should I do—how should I act now, this very day if I could clutch my own pain, and compel it to silence, and think of those three!'
>
> It had taken long for her to come to that question, and there was light piercing into the room. She opened her curtains, and looked out towards the bit of road that lay in view, with fields beyond, outside the entrance-gates. On the road there was a man with a bundle on his back and a woman carrying her baby; in the field she could see figures moving—perhaps the shepherd with his dog. Far off in the bending sky was the pearly light; and she felt the largeness of the world and the manifold wakings of men to labour and endurance. She was a part of that involuntary, palpitating life, and could neither look out on it from her luxurious shelter as a mere spectator, nor hide her eyes in selfish complaining.

The common people do not appear more appositely in many a Marxist novel, and it is worth considering how much emphasis should be placed on this sudden vision. The man and the woman may simply be going to work, or they may have been displaced by national events. Vague though the indication is, it reminds us of the other-directed lives of Romola and St Theresa; Dorothea can only do right by making an effort to join that larger world of 'labour and endurance'. She rejects the inheritance from Casaubon in the same way that Esther rejected the backward-looking Transomes and their estate; and we are told in Chapter 84 that she will go to London and 'live in a street'—a prospect which horrifies Celia. Her new husband represents the consciousness of post-Reform England, and the movement from the country to the town is the way the political balance is going to shift; the parallel to the movement from Warwickshire to London in George Eliot's own life cannot be left out of account either. Dorothea may not herself have been able to do very much, the Finale tells us; but when it came to the crisis she 'spoke for England' and chose the Future instead of the Past.

Nottingham Castle set on fire in the Reform riots of 1832

Prose extract: *Felix in action*

Felix was perfectly conscious that he was in the midst of a tangled business. But he had chiefly before his imagination the horrors that might come if the mass of wild chaotic desires and impulses around him were not diverted from any further attack on places where they would get in the midst of intoxicating and inflammable materials. It was not a moment in which a spirit like his could calculate the effect of misunderstanding as to himself: nature never makes men who are at once energetically sympathetic and minutely calculating. He believed he had the power, and he was resolved to try, to carry the dangerous mass out of mischief till the military came to awe them—which he supposed, from Mr Crow's announcement long ago, must be a near event.

He was followed the more willingly, because Tiliot's Lane was seen by the hindmost to be now defended by constables, some of whom had fire-arms; and where there is no strong counter-movement, any proposition to do something unspecified stimulates stupid curiosity. To many of the Sproxton men who were within sight of him, Felix was known personally, and vaguely believed to be a man who meant many queer things, not at all of an every-day kind. Pressing along like a leader, with the sabre in his hand, and inviting them to bring on Spratt, there seemed a better reason for following him than for doing anything else. A man with a definite will and an energetic personality acts as a sort of flag to draw and bind together the foolish units of a mob. It was on this sort of influence over men whose mental state was a mere medley of appetites and confused impressions, that Felix had dared to count. He hurried them along with words of invitation, telling them to hold up Spratt and not drag him; and those behind followed him, with a growing belief that he had some design worth knowing, while those in front were urged along partly by the same notion, partly by the sense that there was a motive in those behind them, not knowing what the motive was. It was that mixture of pushing forward and being pushed forward, which is a brief history of most human things.

What Felix really intended to do, was to get the crowd by the nearest way out of the town, and induce them to skirt it on the north side with him, keeping up in them the idea that he was leading them to execute some stratagem by which they would surprise something worth attacking, and circumvent the constables who were defending the lanes. In the meantime he trusted that the soldiers would have arrived and with this sort of mob, which was animated by no real political passion or fury against social distinctions, it was in the highest degree unlikely that there would be any resistance to a military force. The presence of fifty soldiers would probably be enough to scatter the rioting hundreds. How numerous the mob was, no one ever knew: many inhabitants afterwards were ready to swear that there must have been at least two thousand rioters. Felix knew he was incurring great risks; but 'his blood was up:' we hardly allow enough in common life for the results of that enkindled passionate enthusiasm which, under other conditions, makes world-famous deeds.

Ch. 33, pp. 427–8

CONTEXT Felix Holt has allowed himself to be drawn into the election riot at Treby Magna. To an outside observer he would now appear to be its leader, having just downed a constable and seized his sabre. In fact he has deliberately assumed the rôle of leader in order to save life and property, and his intention is to draw the crowd of rioters away from the centre of the town. Spratt is 'the hated manager of the Sproxton Colliery', and the intended victim of the mob.

NARRATIVE STYLE George Eliot is not really describing what happened in the manner appropriate to a scene of uproar and violence. Everything is muted, because she is also examining the thoughts in Felix's mind and in the mind of the crowd. A further complication, to be seen in 'tangled business' and 'misunderstanding', is that she is also conscious of what he must appear to be to an unprejudiced witness—a criminal.

MIXED MOTIVES OF THE AUTHOR Felix Holt, who is described as a Radical, is also a kind of conservative. The imagination of the author, in my opinion, sees him as leading the people, but a counter-tendency within her cannot allow him to *actually* lead the assault on privilege which would naturally follow from his ideas. There is therefore a situation akin to nightmare, in which the dreamer performs violent or unnatural actions while the daytime consciousness disapproves. Whether this analogy is helpful or not, the scene is shot through with confused insights and strange reservations, as if in some way Felix, who seems to have got away from the restraints previously imposed upon him by the author, could be *right* in the actions which he performs 'under other conditions' (last sentence). Look, for example, at the way in which the crowd are described by the author as a 'dangerous mass' and a 'mob' in the first two paragraphs: then, in the middle of the third paragraph is the statement that this mob was 'animated by no real political passion or fury against social distinctions'. If they had been, the author says, they would have stood up to the soldiers; but her phrasing could be read as implying that a genuinely revolutionary mob would be a fitter setting for Felix as leader, with 'that enkindled passionate enthusiasm which . . . makes world-famous deeds'.

Prose extract: A meditation upon the life of Saint Theresa

Who that cares much to know the history of man, and how the mysterious mixture behaves under the varying experiments of Time, has not dwelt, at least briefly, on the life of Saint Theresa, has not smiled with some gentleness at the thought of the little girl walking forth one morning hand-in-hand with her still smaller brother, to go and seek martyrdom in the country of the Moors? Out they toddled from rugged Avila, wide-eyed and helpless-looking as two fawns, but with human hearts, already beating to a national idea; until domestic reality met them in the shape of uncles, and turned them back from their great resolve. That child-pilgrimage was a fit beginning. Theresa's passionate, ideal nature demanded an epic life: what were many-volumed romances of chivalry and the social conquests of a brilliant girl to her? Her flame quickly burned up that light fuel; and, fed from within, soared after some illimitable satisfaction, some object which would never justify weariness, which would reconcile self-despair with the rapturous consciousness of life beyond self. She found her epos in the reform of a religious order.

That Spanish woman who lived three hundred years ago was certainly not the last of her kind. Many Theresas have been born who found for themselves no epic life wherein there was a constant unfolding of far-resonant action; perhaps only a life of mistakes, the offspring of a certain spiritual grandeur ill-matched with the meanness of opportunity; perhaps a tragic failure which found no sacred poet and sank unwept into oblivion. With dim lights and tangled circumstance they tried to shape their thought and deed in noble agreement; but after all, to common eyes their struggles seemed mere inconsistency and formlessness; for these later-born Theresas were helped by no coherent social faith and order which could perform the function of knowledge for the ardently willing soul. Their ardour alternated between a vague ideal and the common yearning of womanhood; so that the one was disapproved as extravagance, and the other condemned as a lapse.

Some have felt that these blundering lives are due to the inconvenient indefiniteness with which the Supreme Power has fashioned the natures of women: if there were one level of feminine incompetence as strict as the ability to count three and no more, the social lot of women might be treated with scientific certitude. Meanwhile the indefiniteness remains, and the limits of variation are really much wider than any one would imagine from the sameness of women's coiffure and the favourite love-stories in prose and verse. Here and there a cygnet is reared uneasily among the ducklings in the brown pond, and never finds the living stream in fellowship with its own oary-footed kind. Here and there is born a Saint Theresa, foundress of nothing, whose loving heart-beats and sobs after an unattained goodness tremble off and are dispersed among hindrances, instead of centering in some long-recognizable deed.

Prelude to *Middlemarch*, pp. 25–6

THE FRAME IN WHICH MIDDLEMARCH IS SET This is the Prelude to *Middlemarch*: the same theme is taken up again in the last two paragraphs of the Finale. George Eliot carefully enclosed her novel in a frame of references to Saint Theresa; these take us right away from the nineteenth century, in which the story of the novel is set.

SAINT THERESA George Eliot had become interested in Saint Theresa during the period in which she was writing *The Spanish Gypsy*; her Spanish studies led her to visit Spain in 1866–7. Saint Theresa was born at Avila in 1515; the incident referred to in the first paragraph of the Prelude is taken from the saint's own account of her life (the *Autobiography* is available in several modern translations). The 'heart-beats' in the third paragraph refer to the ecstasy of the saint, whose own heart, in her account, was pierced by a spear of Divine love. The spiritual life is the subject of Saint Theresa's *The Interior Castle*, and it could be said that she is more famous for her mystical union with Christ than for her reform of the Carmelite Order of nuns. George Eliot, as a Positivist, 'edits' the achievements of Saint Theresa, as she did those of Savonarola, into the strictly practical rôle of a reformer.

THE FRAME AS SIGNPOST The Prelude and Finale pick out one theme in the novel, and help us to understand what we should be looking for. On the other hand, it could be said to put forward a 'message' about the destiny of women which the author is not able to convey in the text of the novel itself. Actually there are minor references to this theme in the novel; Dorothea's religiosity and 'self-mortification' are ironically mentioned in the early chapters, and on pages 112–3 there is an indication that she has read about Saint Theresa. On pages 594–5 Dorothea plans a 'colony' which she herself would direct, and this is the nearest she comes to founding anything; it would not of course have been an overseas colony but an agricultural settlement like the Chartist colonies of the 1840s. This idea is never allowed to develop and is dismissed by Celia as one of Dodo's 'plans'. There seems therefore to be a discordance between the author's voice in the Prelude *telling* us about her theme, and what the text of the novel *shows* us as the characters begin to act. Certainly a good deal of the Prelude could be read with an ironical edge to the voice; one is invited to 'smile with gentleness' at the early episode in the life of the saint, but by the second paragraph 'common eyes' can only see 'inconsistency and formlessness' which leads to the consideration of 'blundering lives' in the third. Nevertheless, the tone of the whole passage is that of genuine concern for women in the nineteenth century.

THE IMPLIED REMEDY The second paragraph of the Prelude states that 'later-born Theresas' have 'no coherent social faith and order' to help them. The word *order* seems to carry over from the first paragraph the meaning of a religious order in addition to the general idea of some kind of authoritarian discipline; so that what is being lamented is the absence of a directed Catholic organisation which would take control of such unformed lives as Dorothea's. This reminds us of Romola, whose ability to make a success of her life depended in part on the influence of religious authority, personified in the Dominican Savonarola. We remember too how Maggie Tulliver, an obvious 'cygnet... reared uneasily among the ducklings', was at least helped to endure by reading *The Imitation of Christ*. This seems at first to be an unexpected change of direction for a writer like George Eliot, with the emphasis she had picked up from her Evangelical training, which required individuals to make their own moral decisions; but as a Positivist she would have learned from Comte that the structures and organisation of medieval Catholicism were to be admired, though not its supernatural beliefs.

CONCLUSION Both Felix and Dorothea, in spite of their totally different situations, are born out of their due time and cannot fully engage with the society in which they find themselves. As opposed to the Positivist Romance of *Romola*, the novel of *Middlemarch* will consider at some length how such people adjust to or are beaten down by the world. For a girl like Dorothea, there is offered the possibility of marriage as a way of acting out her aspirations; this is what will lead her to make a surprising choice.

10 Constructing *Middlemarch*

Middlemarch is a reflective rather than an immediately exciting book, and its gestation was prolonged. It consists of several stories, and their interweaving is complex. This is not to say that there is any particular merit in entangling and then disentangling a series of narratives; this can be seen to take place in any long serial such as *The Archers* or *Coronation Street*. In George Eliot's novel the complexity of the narrative structure must be understood as part of the intention announced on the title page—to provide 'a study of provincial life'. It is a book which works by a slow process of accumulation as the themes of the different stories reinforce one another; it is also a very even book, from which one could not select 'best bits' with any confidence. It therefore comes as rather a surprise, when we look at the history of its composition, to see how many changes took place between the first thoughts and the final version.

A certain amount of evidence is available for detailed study of the origin of *Middlemarch*, though there are gaps where additional material would be useful if it had survived. George Eliot kept notes of her reading, and one notebook is described as the 'quarry' for the novel, from which the finished work could be thought of as being 'hewn'. The 'quarry' consists of two main sections: the first contains notes on medical subjects, and on the years 1829–32; the second enables us to follow the planning of the novel in some detail. For example, we can find additional information, such as the titles originally given to the chapters (suppressed in the text of the novel) and also factual notes about the ages of the characters; the 'quarry' also contains a little diagram—one can hardly call it a map—showing the location of the villages mentioned in the story.

In 1869 George Eliot thought of writing a novel about a medical man who would live in a town called Middlemarch; it began with the Vincys and Mr Featherstone. After a time this plan was abandoned, and at the end of 1870 we hear she has begun work on a new novel, to be called *Miss Brooke*. In 1871 she joined the two narratives together. *Middlemarch* began to appear as a part-work from December 1871; it ran until December 1872. Though it is hardly necessary to make allowances for the conditions of serial publication, as one has to do in the case of Dickens, it is important to realise that the interest of readers in the different sets of characters had to be retained over a long period. Finally, the complete work was issued in *four* volumes, which was a new concept in the age of the three-volume novel. Though this point may seem trivial, it is important to bear in mind when meeting the criticism that *Middlemarch* is a conventional work.

Because of twentieth-century misconceptions it is very easy for us to misunderstand what George Eliot is trying to do in her 'study of provincial life'. The characters are taken from widely separated social classes, and in this way an attempt is made to represent the whole society, and to show how one class depends upon another; George Eliot is also concerned with 'the stealthy convergence of human lots' (p. 122), and the unexpected conjunctions between them. Middlemarch is modelled upon the industrial town of Coventry, but it is best to forget the traditional notion of a nineteenth-century industrial town with a mass of factory hands and a few employers. As John Prest points out in a monograph entitled *The Industrial Revolution in Coventry*, social relations in that town were comparatively backward, because the principal industry, that of ribbon-manufacture, was carried on by a number of small masters: 'in 1830 Coventry still epitomised the old order, in which there were many ranks and conditions of men within a single homogeneous society.' Most novels have difficulty enough in showing the social relations possible within one class of people, and George Eliot's problem in constructing her novel may be summarised as follows: in real life the various 'ranks and conditions of men' in a town like Coventry and its surrounding county would have kept themselves to themselves. Ignoring purely fortuitous meetings, they would only have encountered each other on business or on occasions involving some form of social ritual. Luckily these are of interest to this novelist, and we have many accounts of the work undertaken by the doctor, the banker, the clergyman and the land-agent; we are also invited, as it were, to dinner-parties and to meetings of the hospital board, besides the more populous political scenes. Such meetings, however, only serve to bring out the more superficial aspects of human character, and the novelist is principally interested in deeper layers of the personality. Meetings in which these depths are revealed can hardly be imagined. To take an example, in no circumstances in real life would a county 'lady' like Dorothea have called upon a tradesman's daughter like Rosamond Vincy; George Eliot goes to considerable lengths to make this clear, and yet the visit does take place convincingly in the novel. George Eliot has to exercise immense skill to weave together the stories of widely separated social groups and to make the final result believable.

Mr Brooke's dinner-parties in Book I illustrate both aspects of what we have been considering—the separateness of the classes and the novelist's skill in linking them together. Brooke is a member of the landed gentry and would naturally associate only with his equals, that is 'the small group of gentry with whom he visited in the north east of Loamshire' (p. 33)—to visit with, as in US English, means 'exchanged visits'. At the dinner-party in Chapter 3, Sir James Chettam and Mr Casaubon are present because they are gentlemen; whatever is said about his learning Casaubon would not have been there at all if he were a poor scholar—in fact he is very rich and lives in 'a considerable mansion with much land attached to it. The parsonage was inhabited by the curate' (p. 74). In Chapter 6 we encounter Mrs Cadwallader, 'a lady of immeasurably high birth'; she is an exaggerated character, but it is wrong to see her only as a joke figure without noticing how she is used to define and exemplify the unspoken attitudes of the gentry: 'the vulgar rich . . . were no part of God's design in making the world' (p. 84). In spite of her prejudices, we find her in the company of such vulgar people at Brooke's second dinner-party in Chapter 10; there are present 'a manufacturer' (Vincy Senior) and 'a banker' (Bulstrode), together with 'professional men' (Lydgate the surgeon and Standish the lawyer, for example). Mrs Cadwallader can explain this by observing that Brooke is 'beginning to treat the Middlemarchers' (p. 114); she means that there is no sincerity in his invitations and he is preparing for the business side of a Parliamentary election by a conspicuous display in entertainment. The author's voice at the top of page 115 confirms John Prest's social analysis:

> in that part of the country, before Reform had done its notable part in developing the political consciousness, there was a clearer distinction of ranks and a dimmer distinction of parties.

Brooke is therefore seen as exceptionally lax in his 'miscellaneous' gathering, in which the true gradation of provincial society is temporarily obscured: when Lydgate is singled out as a 'gentleman' Lady Chettam is quite put out—'For my part, I like a medical man more on a footing with the servants' (p. 117).

The dinner-party is followed by an essay on social mobility, which is worth pondering; it is at the beginning of Chapter 11 (pp. 122–4). In spite of the jokes significant points are made. 'Squires and baronets, and even lords' are beginning to mix with the citizens of Middlemarch, but they are becoming divided; within the town the Vincys are now regarded as 'old manufacturers' and therefore a cut above Bulstrode, who, although wealthy, 'was not born in the town'. These 'nice [i.e. exact] distinctions of rank in Middlemarch' are further explored on pages 262–4, where we learn that the Vincys would not have associated with the Garths were it not for the accident of 'Mr Featherstone's double marriage (the first to Mr Garth's sister, and the second to Mrs Vincy's)'.

Having considered the wider gulfs in provincial society and the 'nice distinctions', we have now to examine how the novelist knits

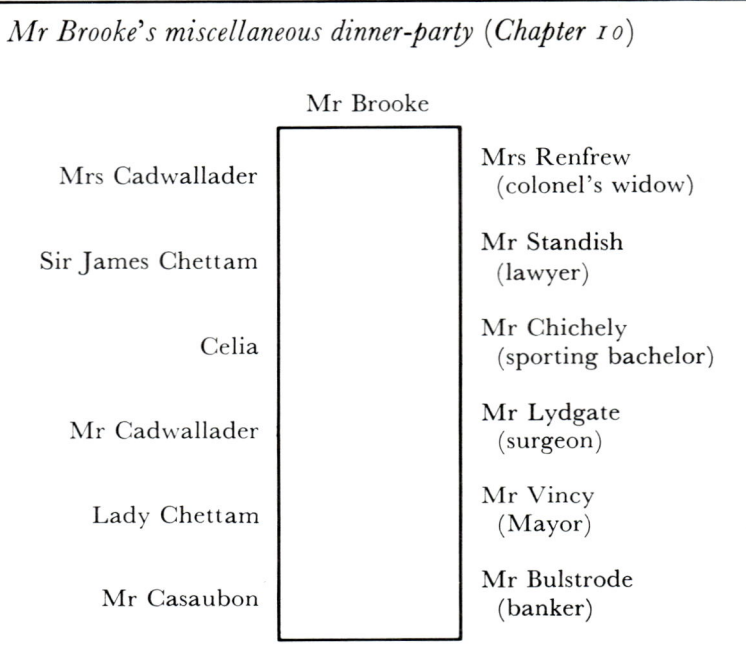

Mr Brooke's miscellaneous dinner-party (Chapter 10)

Mr Brooke

Mrs Cadwallader — Mrs Renfrew (colonel's widow)

Sir James Chettam — Mr Standish (lawyer)

Celia — Mr Chichely (sporting bachelor)

Mr Cadwallader — Mr Lydgate (surgeon)

Lady Chettam — Mr Vincy (Mayor)

Mr Casaubon — Mr Bulstrode (banker)

Dorothea

Note: Those on the left are the landowners and gentry from the County of Loamshire. On the right are the Middlemarchers i.e. representatives of the trade and the professions from the town of Middlemarch; Mrs Renfrew's standing in these two different worlds is not exactly clear from the text, but of course her own status derives from her late husband's profession.

Some relationships in Middlemarch (*notice the link at Harriet Bulstrode*)

A. *Featherstone's Web*:

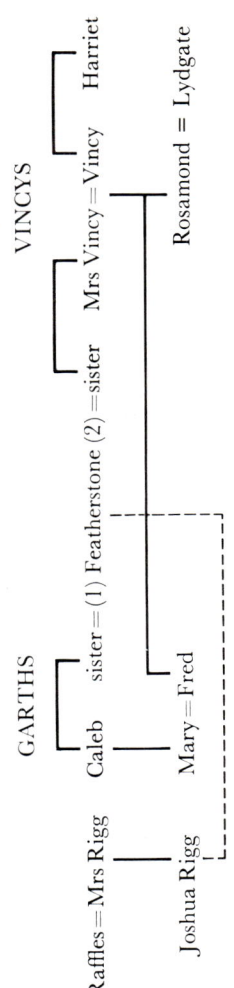

B. *Ladislaw's ancestry*

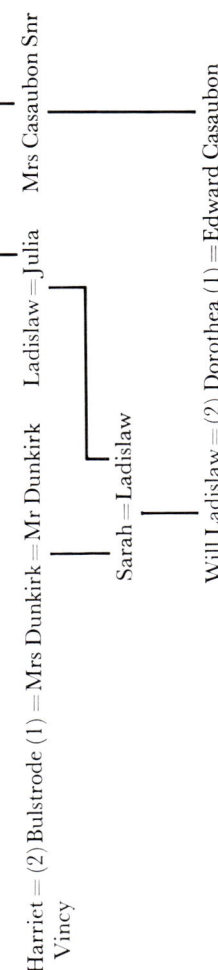

Manuscript page from Middlemarch; *opening of Chapter 1*

the different ranks together in her full-scale study of the provincial society which Middlemarch provides. It is natural to use the metaphor of 'weaving', and George Eliot seems to support this with her constant use of the term 'web'. We could then describe the construction of the novel in the same terms, a weaving together of different strands represented by stories, characters and themes. In fact, the metaphor seems to be quite opposite in its intention; for example, in the famous passage in Chapter 15 she says:

> I at least have so much to do in *unravelling* certain human lots, and seeing how they *were woven* and interwoven, that all the light I can command must be concentrated on this particular web....
>
> p. 170 (my italics)

The same word is used in discussing Lydgate's and Bichat's researches on p. 177, the search for 'the primary webs' out of which human tissue is made. Of course George Eliot is totally responsible for the construction of her book, and therefore it is quite reasonable to think of the web as something which she weaves as she goes along, but this is not what the passage above tells us. There the author's voice comes from the darkness where she is working, saying that she is trying to *undo* a fabric *which is already in existence*. The author could then be described as a Sybil or Norn, interpreting a web woven from the beginning of the world by fate or destiny; this interpretation would support a deterministic view of human life—and for many readers *Middlemarch* is a depressing book because characters like Lydgate seem unable to break free from a predetermined fate. The author sees herself as not being in control of the entire text; her powers are limited to those of a partial seer, who can tell us only what she is able to make out. As I have already hinted in discussing the passages about Arthur Donnithorne and Felix Holt, this seems to me a more interesting authorial voice than the totally dominating presence which is all that some readers are able to detect.

Prose extract: The two sisters

> The casket was soon open before them, and the various jewels spread out, making a bright parterre on the table. It was no great collection, but a few of the ornaments were really of remarkable beauty, the finest that was obvious at first being a necklace of purple amethysts set in exquisite gold-work, and a pearl cross with five brilliants in it. Dorothea immediately took up the necklace and fastened it round her sister's neck, where it fitted almost as closely as a bracelet; but the circle suited the Henrietta-Maria style of Celia's head and neck, and she could see that it did, in the pier-glass opposite.

There, Celia! you can wear that with your Indian muslin. But this cross you must wear with your dark dresses.'

Celia was trying not to smile with pleasure. 'O Dodo, you must keep the cross yourself.'

No, no, dear, no,' said Dorothea, putting up her hand with careless deprecation.

'Yes, indeed you must; it would suit you—in your black dress, now,' said Celia, insistingly. 'You *might* wear that.'

'Not for the world, not for the world. A *cross* is the last thing I would wear as a trinket.' Dorothea shuddered slightly.

'Then you will think it wicked in me to wear it,' said Celia, uneasily.

'No, dear, no,' said Dorothea, stroking her sister's cheek. 'Souls have complexions too: what will suit one will not suit another.'

'But you might like to keep it for mamma's sake.'

'No, I have other things of mamma's—her sandal-wood box, which I am so fond of—plenty of things. In fact, they are all yours, dear. We need discuss them no longer. There—take away your property.'

Celia felt a little hurt. There was a strong assumption of superiority in this Puritanic toleration, hardly less trying to the blond flesh of an unenthusiastic sister than a Puritanic persecution.

'But how can I wear ornaments if you, who are the elder sister, will never wear them?'

'Nay, Celia, that is too much to ask, that I should wear trinkets to keep you in countenance. If I were to put on such a necklace as that, I should feel as if I had been pirouetting. The world would go round with me, and I should not know how to walk.'

Celia had unclasped the necklace and drawn it off. 'It would be a little tight for your neck; something to lie down and hang would suit you better,' she said, with some satisfaction. The complete unfitness of the necklace from all points of view for Dorothea, made Celia happier in taking it. She was opening some ring-boxes, which disclosed a fine emerald with diamonds, and just then the sun passing beyond a cloud sent a bright gleam over the table.

'How very beautiful these gems are!' said Dorothea, under a new current of feeling, as sudden as the gleam. 'It is strange how deeply colours seem to penetrate one, like scent. I suppose that is the reason why gems are used as spiritual emblems in the Revelation of St John. They look like fragments of heaven. I think that emerald is more beautiful than any of them.'

'And there is a bracelet to match it,' said Celia. 'We did not notice this at first.'

'They are lovely,' said Dorothea, slipping the ring and bracelet on her finely-turned finger and wrist, and holding them towards the window on a level with her eyes. All the while her thought was trying to justify her delight in the colours by merging them in her mystic religious joy.

'You *would* like those, Dorothea,' said Celia, rather falteringly, beginning to think with wonder that her sister showed some weakness, and also that emeralds would suit her own complextion even better than purple amethysts. 'You must keep that ring and bracelet—if nothing else. But see, these agates are very pretty—and quiet.'

'Yes! I will keep these—this ring and bracelet,' said Dorothea. Then, letting her hand fall on the table, she said in another tone—'Yet what miserable men find such things, and work at them, and sell them!' She paused again, and Celia thought that her sister was going to renounce the ornaments, as in consistency she ought to do.

'Yes, dear, I will keep these,' said Dorothea, decidedly. 'But take all the rest away, and the casket.'

She took up her pencil without removing the jewels, and still looking at them. She thought of often having them by her, to feed her eye at these little fountains of pure colour.

'Shall you wear them in company?' said Celia, who was watching her with real curiosity as to what she would do.

Dorothea glanced quickly at her sister. Across all her imaginative adornment of those whom she loved, there darted now and then a keen discernment, which was not without a scorching quality. If Miss Brooke ever attained perfect meekness, it would not be for lack of inward fire.

'Perhaps,' she said, rather haughtily. 'I cannot tell to what level I may sink.'

Middlemarch, Ch. 1, pp. 34–6

CONTEXT The extract comes from the very first chapter of the novel, and establishes that the relationship between these two sisters may be regarded as one of gentle rivalry. The first part of the chapter, continuing from the mood of the Prelude, was narrative; it was largely concerned with Dorothea, who was taken seriously, but also subjected to ironical asides. Like Maggie, Dorothea is vaguely High Church; she is associated with 'the Blessed Virgin' on the first page of the novel (p. 29), and in spite of her Puritan ancestry and dress she is suspected of 'fasting like a Papist' (p. 31). Unlike Maggie, Dorothea is gently mocked by the author: there is a particularly good paragraph about her matrimonial expectations on page 32, ending with the sentence:

The really delightful marriage must be that where your husband was a sort of father, and could teach you even Hebrew, if you wished it.

It is clear that we are not to be enveloped in Dorothea's consciousness as we were in Maggie's. Celia, on the other hand, is cast as the sensible but limited person who always brings the idealist in Dorothea down to earth; she is very perceptive about the things of this world. She wishes to divide the contents of their mother's jewel-box.

TONE In the extract the chapter changes from narrative to dramatic presentation, and the mood changes to comedy. At first we are made to witness a duel of words which Dorothea wins; indeed, some of her remarks could be described as positively intended to put down Celia as a 'little silly', were it not for the fact that the author makes it clear that Dorothea is overdoing it—'careless deprecation', 'shuddered slightly', and 'assumption of superiority'. Quite suddenly the mood changes, as the sun 'passing beyond a cloud sent a bright gleam over the table'; this seems to release in Dorothea 'a new current of feeling, as sudden as the gleam'. It is as if the superior 'reasons' were subtly undermined from within; Dorothea is forced to acknowledge the beauty and the strangeness of the jewels—one thinks of Wordsworth and 'the visionary gleam' or perhaps 'the light that never was on land or sea'—'It is strange how deeply colours seem to penetrate one, like scent.' Dorothea is temporarily thrown into a state of ecstasy, which her 'thought' is behindhand in 'trying to justify'. Finally she comes round from this nearly trance-like state, and by the end of the extract has quite recovered herself.

SYMBOLISM While the scene is successful simply on account of the beauty of the gems, and the way in which they are attuned to Dorothea's 'mystic religious joy', it is only fair to point out that in many Victorian novels jewels symbolise sex. (Diamonds, which Grandcourt gives to his mistress and then to his wife, bear a deeper significance in *Daniel Deronda*, and drive Gwendolen into a fit of hysteria.) Here something far more gentle is signified; the wearing of the dead mother's jewels signifies the acceptance of the rôle of an adult, and implies their use in attracting a sexual partner. Dorothea's choice in marriage will be the theme of the next chapters of the novel.

11 Character in *Middlemarch*

George Eliot's method of displaying character in her novel is complex. It is also slow-moving: 'character is a process and an unfolding', as the author informs us on page 178. Therefore it is never wise to take any statement about one of the major figures in the novel too 'finally', even when it is apparently a judgement given by George Eliot. In this novel the author hovers above the text, inserting her opinions and guiding us in certain directions; and though she enters into the consciousness of different characters from time to time, she is quite capable of suddenly withdrawing her sympathy, and this can be confusing, especially if we are used to novels written from only a single point of view. Like all novelists, she changes from narrative to dramatisation when she needs to show her characters in action. As we saw in the extract from the first chapter, a dramatic scene may serve to develop the character and open up a possibility which had hitherto been hidden from us; 'character is not cut in marble', as Mr Farebrother wisely observes (p. 790). With this in mind it seems worth looking for examples of unexpected behaviour in the novel, and considering how our attitude to the characters is changed.

George Eliot's presentation of Mr Casaubon is often difficult to appreciate when we read the novel for the first time. He is remarkably unattractive, and it is easy to fall into the error of assuming that unattractive characters are dully imagined because the author presents them as dull and unimaginative. In fact, as we shall see, Casaubon is treated by the author with extreme sensitivity. We are also led astray by the fact that we see him from Dorothea's point of view, assisted by wry remarks from Mrs Cadwallader and the author herself. At first it is only too easy to misread the situation; the relationship of Dorothea and Casaubon looks like a realistic version of one of the most widespread folk stories of all time—the marriage of January and May. As in Chaucer's 'Merchant's Tale', we assume that Casaubon will be mocked because he is ridiculous, impotent and old, and that Dorothea will soon turn to a new lover—Will Ladislaw is waiting in the wings. But this is a different story. Dorothea is not forced into a marriage, nor does she marry the older man for his money as in the classic story. She chooses to marry Casaubon because he is attractive to her, and she rejects her younger suitor, Sir James Chettam, in his favour. The heart of the matter is her disillusionment with him; he has to live up to her naïve expectations, not only about marriage but about human life.

Because Casaubon never seems likely to finish his book, and in the end never does finish it, it is too easy to brand him as a failure. It is true that he fails in his quest for the key to all mythologies, but like many great Victorians he did act on the assumption that there are simple unifying principles behind superficially disparate phenomena. The key to all mythologies did appear at the end of the century as Sir James Frazer's *The Golden Bough*; and one must remember that G. H. Lewes spent years trying to apply science and philosophy to solve 'problems of life and mind', and that Herbert Spencer wished to systematise human knowledge.

Casaubon is lost, and he is ill; just the sort of person whom a modern St Theresa might wish to succour and prop. But the image for their relationship is more appropriately to be found in pagan mythology. Casaubon's failure of direction is symbolised by the labyrinth—the word 'labyrinthine' is used twice in establishing his character (p. 46). There is a long dissection of his feelings at the beginning of Chapter 10, and the enduring picture of Casaubon exploring the vaults with a taper is set before us. The oil in his lamp which Dorothea expected to find is contrasted with the 'dryness' of the bridegroom postulated by Mrs Cadwallader (p. 117). Once at Rome Dorothea is immediately 'placed' in conjunction with the statue of Ariadne—Ariadne who gave Theseus the clue or 'key' to the labyrinth and was abandoned by him. Casaubon does not really need her help with his research, and the labyrinth image becomes actual among the real ruins of Rome; Dorothea is unable to follow him (pp. 228–30).

Another chain of imagery presents the grand aspirations of Dorothea as a 'lake' (p. 47) or the 'sea' (p. 228): in fact the marriage locks her in to 'an enclosed basin' (p. 228). We begin to assume that the author is firmly on Dorothea's side in all this, but at the beginning of Chapter 29 George Eliot suddenly reverses the viewpoint: 'Was her point of view the only possible one with regard to this marriage?' We are then given a sympathetic but qualified account of Casaubon's feelings. What is to be found at the centre of his personality is 'a small hungry shivering self'. The balance begins to tilt towards Casaubon, in spite of his pettiness and his jealousy of Will Ladislaw; in his last illness, stripped of his pretensions, he reaches out to universal status as he faces death with dignity. He goes ahead of Dorothea, and of Lydgate, and of all of us, down the Yew-Tree Walk whose symbolism is too obvious to need commenting on.

While it is possible to applaud the presentation of Casaubon as a finished sculpture in the round, clearly there in the reader's mind, the opposite is true of Will Ladislaw. He is an outsider, and upsets the established prejudices of Middlemarch—he is described at the auction as 'a fellow with low designs' (p. 651). This is one of the rare occasions in the novel when he is shown apart from Dorothea;

normally we are forced to look at him through her eyes. For this reason we may feel that the author regards him too kindly, and forgets to include him in her general irony. For example, he is meant to appear as a foil to Casaubon. He has the unfair advantages of youth and of physical attractiveness, so that when we read that

> the first impression of seeing Will was one of sunny brightness ... Mr Casaubon, on the contrary, stood rayless....
>
> p. 241

it is hardly to be described as a 'joke' or an 'irony' or anything so subtle. One feels sympathy for Casaubon. However, if we read the passage as representing *Dorothea's* perception of the scene, then the author is simply indicating how the two men appeared to a woman who is unconsciously beginning to choose between them. But it remains very difficult for us, as impartial readers, to get Ladislaw into focus. He is so easily confused with his 'image' in Dorothea's eyes.

An example of this is his discovery at Rosamond's house by Dorothea:

> 'Perhaps I have been mistaken in many things,' said poor Dorothea to herself, while the tears came rolling and she had to dry them quickly. She felt confusedly unhappy, and the image of Will which had been so clear to her before was mysteriously spoiled.
>
> p. 472

It is possible to justify many of Ladislaw's peculiarities, and they do irritate many readers, by saying that he is a projection of Dorothea's fantasy throughout the book, a point perhaps confirmed by the dreamy but crucial sequence in Chapter 79, as the novel moves to its climax:

> The limit of resistance was reached, and she had sunk back helpless within the clutch of inescapable anguish. Dismissing Tantripp with a few faint words, she locked her door, and turning away from it towards the vacant room she pressed her hands hard on the top of her head, and moaned out—
> 'Oh, I did love him!'
> Then came the hour in which the waves of suffering shook her too thoroughly to leave any power of thought. She could only cry in loud whispers, between her sobs, after her lost belief which she had planted and kept alive from a very little seed since the days in Rome—after her lost joy of clinging with silent love and faith to one who, misprized by others, was worthy in her thought—after her lost woman's pride of reigning in his memory—after her sweet dim perspective of hope, that along some pathway they should meet with unchanged recognition and take up the backward years as a yesterday....

There were two images—two living forms that tore her heart in two, as if it had been the heart of a mother who seems to see her child divided by the sword, and presses one bleeding half to her breast while her gaze goes forth in agony towards the half which is carried away by the lying woman that has never known the mother's pang.

Here, with the nearness of an answering smile, here within the vibrating bond of mutual speech, was the bright creature whom she had trusted—who had come to her like the spirit of morning visiting the dim vault where she sat as the bride of a worn-out life; and now, with a full consciousness which had never awakened before, she stretched out her arms towards him and cried with bitter cries that their nearness was a parting vision: she discovered her passion to herself in the unshrinking utterance of despair.

And there, aloof, yet persistently with her, moving wherever she moved, was the Will Ladislaw who was a changed belief exhausted of hope, a detected illusion—no, a living man towards whom there could not yet struggle any wail of regretful pity, from the midst of scorn and indignation and jealous offended pride.

pp. 844–5

These two views of Ladislaw are also present in *our* minds. At the end of the story we may feel some sympathy for Sir James Chettam, who, in spite of an effort, 'never liked Ladislaw'; but this is to allow the Middlemarchers the victory. In fact Ladislaw must surely be taken as an entirely new kind of person, a professional politician, and also, looking ahead, as a trial run for the character of Daniel Deronda.

One final example of the unexpected in George Eliot's treatment of character may be considered at this point, before we move to an examination of Lydgate and his problems. Bulstrode, like Ladislaw, is an outsider, who achieves financial success and marries Harriet Vincy, the mayor's sister. From the begining of the story his fragile status is clear to the Middlemarchers; 'he's got no land hereabout,' says old Featherstone, 'He may come down any day when the devil leaves off backing him' (p. 138). Though he soon remedies this defect by buying Stone Court when Featherstone is dead, hints are dropped that all has not been right in Bulstrode's past life. When the full narrative of that past is given to us (pp. 663–8), and the eminent 'Christian' is exposed, he becomes, like Mrs Transome, a potentially tragic figure whose fall has been the result of a long 'train of causes' (p. 665). All this, however, serves to bring us to one of the great moments in the novel, when Mrs Bulstrode, of whom we expect very little, finds the moral courage to stand by her husband in his disgrace (pp. 806–8). The way in which this inconspicuous character earns our respect illustrates the unexpectedness of behaviour which speaks out against a totally predetermined sequence of events; it both illustrates the 'earned' right to teach morality for which this author is famous, and also prepares us for the surprises in her next novel.

Prose extract: The hospital vote

'Gentlemen,' said Mr Bulstrode, in a subdued tone, 'the merits of the question may be very briefly stated, and if any one present doubts that every gentleman who is about to give his vote has not been fully informed, I can now recapitulate the considerations that should weigh on either side'.

'I don't see the good of that,' said Mr Hawley. 'I suppose we all know whom we mean to vote for. Any man who wants to do justice does not wait till the last minute to hear both sides of the question. I have no time to lose, and I propose that the matter be put to the vote at once.'

A brief but still hot discussion followed before each person wrote 'Tyke' or 'Farebrother' on a piece of paper and slipped it into a glass tumbler; and in the meantime Mr Bulstrode saw Lydgate enter.

'I perceive that the votes are equally divided at present,' said Mr Bulstrode, in a clear biting voice. Then, looking up at Lydgate—

'There is a casting-vote still to be given. It is yours, Mr Lydgate: will you be good enough to write?'

'The thing is settled now,' said Mr Wrench, rising. 'We all know how Mr Lydgate will vote.'

'You seem to speak with some peculiar meaning, sir,' said Lydgate, rather defiantly, and keeping his pencil suspended.

'I merely mean that you are expected to vote with Mr Bulstrode. Do you regard that meaning as offensive?'

'It may be offensive to others. But I shall not desist from voting with him on that account.'

Lydgate immediately wrote down 'Tyke'.

So the Rev. Walter Tyke became chaplain to the Infirmary, and Lydgate continued to work with Mr Bulstrode. He was really uncertain whether Tyke were not the more suitable candidate, and yet his consciousness told him that if he had been quite free from indirect bias he should have voted for Mr Farebrother. The affair of the chaplaincy remained a sore point in his memory as a case in which this petty medium of Middlemarch had been too strong for him. How could a man be satisfied with a decision between such alternatives and under such circumstances? No more than he can be satisfied with his hat, which he has chosen from among such shapes as the resources of the age offer him, wearing it at best with a resignation which is chiefly supported by comparison.

Middlemarch, Ch. 18, pp. 216–17

CONTEXT A vote is to be taken at the hospital board. Either Mr Farebrother or Mr Tyke is to have the post of chaplain. Lydgate is a friend of Farebrother's and knows how much he could do with the salary. But he is indebted to Bulstrode for his own post of medical superintendent at the hospital, and Tyke is Bulstrode's nominee. For all Lydgate's deluded belief in his ability to think and act independently, he is seen by others as Bulstrode's creature. Lydgate is unable to overcome what he regards as the 'petty medium of Middlemarch'.

LYDGATE'S TRAGEDY Lydgate's path through the novel is that of a falling arrow; potentially, he has everything necessary to make a success of his life, but his actual achievements are negligible. The problem is whether he is to be taken as one of George Eliot's predetermined characters, whether in fact he is destroyed from without or within. In this the passage is ambiguous, the last meditative paragraph beginning within his consciousness—'He was really uncertain . . .'—and then sliding into the voice of the narrator, who concludes with a generalisation about hats. This seems to imply that we can only make our lives out of what 'the resources of the age offer', that we must cut our coat according to the cloth which history makes available.

Lydgate appears to be wound up like a clock. The account of his previous life before coming to Middlemarch, which is given in Chapter 15, anticipates his entire story. There is his 'intellectual passion' (p. 173), and the good intentions of his research; but when we hear of 'middle-aged men . . . packed by the gross' we know Lydgate's destiny, in the same way that the adventure with Laure prefigures his relationships with women. On the final page of the chapter, the image of Middlemarch 'swallowing' and 'assimilating him very comfortably' (p. 183) leaves nothing at all for our comfort. Those who find *Middlemarch* a depressing book point to such things: there is no escape, every good intention is eventually dissipated, every sapling grows into a tree which will one day fall to the ground.

Lydgate, it seems, can never win. He is tested and found wanting at the hospital vote: 'the petty medium of Middlemarch had been too strong for him.' He is similarly absorbed by Rosamond:

> Lydgate's [idea of remaining unengaged] lay blind and unconcerned as a jelly-fish which gets melted without knowing it.

After their marriage his appeal to his wife to help clear them of debt (Chapter 58) is comic and tragic at the same time: the way in which the voice of Dorothea is overheard in his mind (p. 638) anticipates the way in which she will save him. Dorothea acts according to the religion of humanity: 'People glorify all sorts of bravery except the bravery they might show on behalf of their nearest neighbours' (p. 791) or 'If we had lost our own chief good, other people's good would remain, and that is worth trying for' (p. 868). In this way she finds a 'channel' (p. 896) for the energies of a St Theresa, and, in visiting Rosamond, learns how she may secure her own happiness.

Lydgate admits to Dorothea: 'I had some ambition. I meant everything to be different with me' (p. 821), but ends up in fashionable practice wearing himself out as Rosamond's slave. He signs off with the remark about the basil plant (p. 893), thinking of Keats's poem, which shows defiance to the last. Nevertheless, the effect of the whole of Lydgate's story needed to be counterbalanced by an example of amelioration and upward growth. This is provided by Fred Vincy, who begins in debt, and is shown as a dull oaf who has not benefited from any 'intellectual passion'—'My education was a mistake' (p. 607). Once he has brought himself to admit this he is prepared to humble himself, to listen to Caleb Garth's good counsel, and to climb slowly up to the rank of country farmer. One of the best scenes in the book takes place in the Billiard-room; Fred sees Lydgate playing, but is just able to resist the temptation to join in and bet (pp. 722–4): on the way up he crosses Lydgate's path on the way down.

12 The achievement of *Middlemarch*

That *Middlemarch* is now regarded as the crown of George Eliot's work is largely the result of the influence of Dr Leavis. It was not always so; to the Victorians she was often simply 'the author of *Romola*'. It was Virginia Woolf who first pointed out that *Middlemarch* is one of the few English novels written for grown-up people'. It is now established as a standard to which all other nineteenth-century novels can be referred and compared.

Henry James, who admired the book only partially, said in his review of *Middlemarch*:

> It sets a limit, we think, to the development of the old-fashioned English novel.

This proposition could be expanded in various ways. In length alone, it would seem that only this novel could stretch the form to such a limit, its different stories united in the theme of the slow attrition of the good intentions of human life. On completing it, one has the impression of having lived through it; in the memory its action seems to take far longer than the two and a half years from September 1829 to May 1832. James is using development, as many Victorians did, with the extra meaning of 'evolution'; in *Middlemarch* a form of intellectual life has reached perfection and must now become extinct. If this is the case, and if George Eliot is to be identified with the form in which she has written, then there would seem to be nothing else left for its author to do. Yet, ignoring the perfection of the form, the ideas which animate the novel still demand resolution. The very first paragraph of the Prelude, summoning up St Theresa, asked for 'the rapturous consciousness of a life beyond self' which the book was never able to grant to Dorothea; and so, as if nothing had advanced on this front at least in the course of the story, the closing paragraphs return to St Theresa, in conjunction with Antigone, lamenting that 'the medium in which their ardent deeds took shape is for ever gone'. The author then brings her book to a reasonable, Positivist and realistic close, claiming that 'the growing good of the world' depends upon those who have no memorial, and whose lives are as if they had never been. But the implied questioning of the scheme of things remains unanswered; the book is not so neatly sewn up as has been supposed.

It is to this unanswered problem that George Eliot returns in *Daniel Deronda*, and astonishes us with the modernity of her choice of subject. For those whom religion can no longer illuminate, only a political cause can call forth similar energies to the faith of the past. To discuss this will demand a new kind of novel.

13 The modernity of *Daniel Deronda*

George Eliot's last novel is in many ways the opposite of what we might have expected. It is experimental, and is set apart from her earlier work, so that it could almost be a first novel by a different writer. The most obvious change is that it is contemporary in its subject-matter; it actually takes place in the 1860s, though this is only emphasised in one or two paragraphs by references to events such as the American Civil War. In the earlier novels the people seemed to grow out of their native soil, but in this novel the main characters are rootless and unsettled: even when the scenes are set in the countryside it appears to have been invaded by raffish townees. Gone too, it seems, is the slow and elaborate machinery of cause and effect which congested *Middlemarch*; instead there is a succession of 'inexplicable' catastrophes and sudden conversions. In sum, it is a novel of indeterminism, which, in a quiet way, undermines and destroys the conventions of Victorian fiction. A *young* book by a middle-aged author, it happens to be in the position of a coda or finale—but then George Eliot did not know it was to be her last novel.

It will be easier to begin, though, with those aspects of the book which are familiar, and which look back to the earlier work. The novel has a double plot, and is easily divisible into two halves. On the one hand there is the story of Gwendolen Harleth and her unhappy marriage to Grandcourt; on the other the strange tale of Daniel Deronda himself. He has been brought up in ignorance of his birth and is drawn towards the unknown world of Judaism by a prophet called Mordecai; Deronda discovers that his real parents were Jews, and finally decides to devote his life to a Zionist project. The handling of the two stories—when one has appreciated what the author intends by such a wide contrast between them—is masterly; they were intended to illuminate each other, and George Eliot resented those who wanted to cut the book up into its two 'halves'; not that this has deterred many famous critics from doing just that.

Some of the characters resemble those in earlier novels, too. Gwendolen herself is perhaps a second attempt at the portrayal of a Mrs Transome, but she is a much stronger personality and is capable of surprising evolutions in order to survive. Having sold herself to the highest bidder in the marriage stakes, she is dragged down into a state of almost clinical depression; from this, it seems, she can only recover by listening to the good advice of Daniel Deronda, a relationship which, as Barbara Hardy observes in the Introduction to the Penguin edition, 'would almost certainly have to come out as more sexual in a modern novel.' In fact, he too is a type we have met before in Tito and Will Ladislaw; an exceedingly attractive young man in his early twenties, he seems very inappropriate as a father-confessor. He is given to saying things like

> for us who have to struggle for our wisdom, the higher life must be a region in which the affections are clad with knowledge.
>
> p. 507

Although I have taken this out of context, it is a fair sample of a kind of wisdom which is unhelpfully profound and profoundly unhelpful; I cannot imagine any young man actually saying this, but then the characters in this novel do not obey the rules. In trying to understand the strangeness of this story, it is well to remember D. H. Lawrence's rebuke to Arnold Bennett:

> all rules of construction hold good only for novels which are copies of other novels. A book which is not a copy of other books has its own construction, and what he calls faults, he being an old imitator, I call characteristics.

As in some of her earlier novels, George Eliot heads each chapter with a little motto or epigraph in prose or verse: she has now ceased to invent 'Old Plays' or other sources for them, and most have been written by the author herself. In some cases they raise interesting questions about the narrative which they precede. For example, the long epigraph to the first chapter begins:

> Men can do nothing without the make-believe of a beginning.

It goes on to challenge assumptions about time in Science and in Poetry, and leaves us with the uncomfortable feeling that though religion has not been mentioned, somebody is laughing at us from a standpoint which is outside normal experience. So the epigraph throws into the ring something more 'real' (in an older and philosophical sense) than that reality with which the Victorian novel, and George Eliot's novels in particular, are supposed to deal. The first page of the first chapter opens with a series of questions; these are then discovered, there having been no quotation marks, to be questions in the mind of Daniel Deronda. He is watching the play at the tables of a 'society' gambling establishment; Gwendolen is observed to be winning, but instead of keeping her gains she goes on to lose everything, while the voice of the croupier is described as that of 'destiny'.

It is a strange opening. Gambling, with its mindless choices and results which cannot be predetermined, is presumably to be taken as a paradigm of human behaviour. We no longer know where we are going, and are uncertain whether effect will follow from cause. References to gambling will recur: for example, we learn that Mr Lassman, a broker, has engaged in disastrous speculations which have wiped out Gwendolen's fortune; her mother says, 'He risked too much' (p. 274), and seems unwilling to make a moral judgement.

The epigraph to the first chapter also implies that one could *begin the story anywhere*, and after a few pages the reader finds that this is not the conventional beginning to a novel at all. He is then forced to retrace the events of the preceding year, both for Gwendolen and for Deronda, and it is not until pages 193 and 268 that the scene described in the first chapter comes round again. Later on in the novel, too, there are other occasions when the narrative seems to get out of order, and some events are later than they should have been in a strict chronology. All this is not simply the result of trying to tell two stories simultaneously; it is more deliberate. The author is aiming to upset the reader's expectations, and to suggest that there is something to be gained by destabilising time itself.

If our perception of time needs readjusting, so too do our views of the reasonable nature of mental activity. Why do people do what they do? The earlier George Eliot would have been ready with moral decisions and determining causes: now she seems to be saying that there is an element of chance, and that we cannot understand other people's minds. On page 321 Gwendolen appears to act

> from that streak of superstition in her ... when lingers in an intense personality even in spite of theory and science.

The author comments further down the page that

> There is a great deal of unmapped country within us which would have to be taken into account in an explanation of our gusts and storms.

George Eliot admits that there is a limit to what we can know, that there are mysteries in the universe and mysteries within ourselves; and so she accepts that, even though she is the author of the text, she does not know everything about her characters.

This uncertainty extends to the ending of the novel. There is no conventional finishing point to the tale; we do not follow the people past the end of the story, as in *Middlemarch*, and we do not know whether we have been given a 'happy ending' or otherwise. We are led to assume that Gwendolen has undergone a conversion, a change of heart of the kind denied to Lydgate or similar predetermined characters in George Eliot's fiction. Our assumption is based on the fact that Gwendolen tells her mother, 'I am going to live,' but we have no way of verifying that this is what happens. It may be a delusion, on Gwendolen's part or our own. Similarly, we are told that Daniel is about to leave for the Holy Land. His trunks are packed 'with a complete equipment for Eastern travel,' but his departure is delayed by the death of Mordecai—which concludes the book. It is not just the unfinishedness that seems so modern, it is deeper than that: each moment of time presents us, like the gambler, with different choices and possibilities. There is no reason to suppose that things will proceed in a logical and ordered way. The future is unknown.

The strangeness of the book is compounded by the author's ventures into the realms of the exotic and the infinite; this may seem a strange way of categorising the other new elements in the book, but so they must have appeared at the time. Judaism and Zionism are clear hard-edged concepts to us, but in the nineteenth century the Jews were not understood any more than the Gypsies, who normally do duty for the 'oriental' in English fiction, and represent a life beyond the rules of everyday experience. In her earlier drama, *The Spanish Gypsy*, the heroine is suddenly confronted by a Gypsy king who claims he is her father; like Deronda, she appears not to have enquired into these important matters before. She joins the band of Gypsies, embracing her true *racial* destiny, and eventually leads her people overseas to found a new state. This is, in embryonic form, the same story as that of the Jewish half of *Daniel Deronda*; both books share the frightening belief that the racial inheritance of an individual can take control of his or her rational mind.

Both Gypsies and Jews were perceived as *races* rather than as individuals, and were also seen as a mysterious intrusion into European life. Zionism had not at that time progressed beyond the idea of a national home for the Jews, and this was so vague a concept that other places than the present area of Israel were considered. It was certainly not a political programme, more a dream which George Eliot's *Daniel Deronda* itself contributed to. She was much influenced by her friend Emanuel Deutsch, who died in 1873; he taught her Hebrew, and helped with her research into the Jewish background of the novel. She prepared herself for *Daniel Deronda* by extensive reading. Her own observations contributed; she visited the synagogue in Frankfurt, and her description of the Cohen family (p. 446) is presumably taken from life.

All this can be misread as a warm interest in the future of the Jews, without considering the fact that she was *using* them for the purposes of her novel. It is fair to point out, as many have done, that *any* visionary movement would have done as the foil to Gwendolen's inward-looking self-absorption. Although subsequent historical events happen to have led to the establishment of the state of Israel, George Eliot and her contemporaries could never have foreseen those events in the 1870s. At that time Zionism did not begin to look like a realisable programme; and she may indeed have chosen it as an example of an impossible creed.

This last point, if accepted, would only serve to strengthen the faith which radiates from the character of Mordecai. He addresses the other characters like an Old Testament prophet. Strictly speaking, such beings are not acceptable in a realistic novel at all, except as the objects of satire. It could easily be argued that the novel in England derives in some sense from the philosophy of John Locke, and that private communication from the deity to an individual is inadmissible. But George Eliot is out to experiment upon her readers; Mordecai is not to be laughed at, and every syllable he utters is pregnant with impossibilities. He upsets every preconception of the nineteenth-century European liberal; he is a genuine visionary, being capable of foretelling the appearance of Deronda; in fact, he seems to summon Deronda to him, and announces that Deronda will be his disciple with whose soul he will blend after death. All this is delivered to us by the author quite uncritically; with Mordecai, George Eliot cheats the reader, operating on levels normally denied to the novelist. We are left in some doubt as to the consistency of all this with the Positivist and scientific beliefs which George Eliot adhered to in real life. But remember that science had moved on since the 1850s; George Eliot would have kept up with the latest ideas through Lewes if not through her own interests. Physicists were already proposing intangible substances such as 'the ether', and George Eliot is on record as believing in 'an invisible continuous cosmos' behind perceived reality. Now we have it; for once 'reality' is seen from *outside* as it were, and seen to be itself a human-derived fiction or make-believe which we impose upon an unknowable universe, then the flood-gates are opened; the 'Realism' of the Victorian novel which seemed so solid is washed away before our eyes. It becomes a merely human construct which is incapable of verification. The whole ideological structure which she had so painstakingly built up in her earlier fiction is demolished in this novel. I cannot myself see that a writer who had advanced as far as this would ever have wanted to write another *Middlemarch* or anything resembling it. She has been compared to Shakespeare—'the female Shakespeare so to speak'; in this novel the female Prospero has broken her staff, and drowned her book.

Part Three
Reference Section

A note on the word 'Original'

For many of the entries in this Reference Section the main interest lies in the fact that they either are or were alleged to be the originals from which George Eliot drew her own pictures of places and people. In some cases this is indicated by names in brackets after the main heading.

George Eliot herself was very put out when people rushed in to 'identify' scenes and portraits in her novels. She explained her reservations in a letter of 19 September 1859, thinking of course of *Adam Bede*:

> *There is not a single portrait in Adam Bede* . . . no one who knew my father would call Adam a portrait of him. . . . Again, Dinah and Seth are *not* my aunt and uncle. . . . The whole course of the story in *Adam Bede*—the descriptions of scenery or houses—the characters—the dialogue—*everything* is a combination from widely sundered elements of experience. . . .
> Treddleston is *not* Ellastone. Hayslope is, with a difference. But no one who is not an artist knows how experience is wrought up in writing any form of poetry. . . .

Of course she is right to say this. It is a very elementary theory of art which assumes that it is possible to literally transcribe reality on to the page, and it is a poor compliment to most artists to congratulate them on being able to do this. So, there are no originals . . . yet, 'Hayslope is, with a difference.'

The word 'original', then, can only be used or understood as shorthand for 'one of the widely sundered elements of experience' referred to in the letter. Nevertheless, I would encourage readers to visit some of the places in the Gazetteer, or to look at old photographs of them. George Eliot did claim to be a 'realist', and she deserves the tribute of our intent looking at that reality, even as, after a hundred or a hundred and fifty years, it begins to go out of existence. In the case of George Eliot's novels, fieldwork pays off, in defiance of schools of criticism which urge us to look at words rather than things. In spite of her statement that she is a poet and not a mere reporter of fact, her imagination is linked to reality by her own theory and practice as a novelist; without her patient observation in the first place how much of what we value in the novels would seem to exist with the solidity of an apprehended and tangible world?

George Eliot's England

Gazetteer

NOTE The names in brackets are those used by George Eliot, mainly in *Adam Bede* and *Scenes of Clerical Life*.

Cambridgeshire

GIRTON. George Eliot contributed to the foundation of Girton College; a sketch of her by Samuel Laurence is kept there.

Derbyshire (Stonyshire).

ASHBOURNE (Oakbourne).

DERBY (Stoniton).

DOVEDALE (Eagledale).

NORBURY (Norbourne). The home of George Evans and the birthplace of Robert Evans was at Roston Common; the cottage can be identified by a plaque saying *Adam Bede Cottage*. A photograph showing its former appearance is in Laski's *George Eliot and her World*.

WIRKSWORTH (Snowfield). For a description see *Adam Bede* pp. 438–9 and 518, where it is referred to as 'that bare heap o' stones as the very crows fly over an' won't stop at.' George Eliot visited her aunt Elisabeth Evans here on 18 June 1840.

Wirksworth is an ancient mining town, and in the nineteenth century had become a dormitory for the workers at the Arkwright Mills at Cromford, which is over the top of the hill to the north. It also had its own businesses, such as the Haarlem lace-works which Samuel Evans managed from 1807.

There are two Methodist chapels. The Ebenezer Wesleyan, now disused, is in Chapel Lane off North End; the fact that there are five or six different denominational chapels in Chapel Lane alone is a reminder of the keen religious life of the last century. The surviving Methodist chapel in St John Street was once called the Bede Memorial Chapel.

Kent

DOVER. George Eliot lodged at 1 Sydney Place in March–April 1855.

Lincolnshire

GAINSBOROUGH (St Ogg's). The setting of many scenes in *The Mill on the Floss* remains convincing; for example, there is still a good deal of nineteenth century warehousing along the east bank of the Trent, on the same side as the town (see p. 183). The Old Hall (p. 182), the town's principal medieval building, is now a Folk Museum, containing a display of dairying equipment which illuminates Hetty's work in *Adam Bede*. A small room off the Tudor Room contains some early-twentieth-century watercolours, showing the warehouses and other old buildings, which are very helpful in imagining what George Eliot must have seen in her short visit in 1859. What is misleading is a traced pencil sketch of a very large industrial building (with maltings behind?) which is equipped with a colossal tower and windmill; this is a traced pencil sketch from an original said to date from 1843. It is entitled 'The Mill on the Floss', but is not connected with the mill in our text. (See further under MISTERTON SOSS below).

LINCOLN (Lindum).

London

George Eliot's residences are listed below in chronological order.

142 Strand (1851–3)
21 Cambridge Street, Hyde Park Square (1853–4)
8 Victoria Grove Terrace, Bayswater (1855)—now Ossington Street
7 Clarence Row, East Sheen (1855)
8 Park Shot, Richmond (1855–8)
Holly Lodge, South Fields, Wandsworth (1859–60)
10 Harewood Square (Sept. 1860)
16 Blandford Square (late 1860–63)
The Priory, 21 North Bank, Regent's Park (1863–80)—now demolished
4 Cheyne Walk, Chelsea (1880)

Both G. H. Lewes and George Eliot are buried in Highgate Cemetery. There is a tablet to George Eliot in Westminster Abbey. Her complete library is at Dr Williams Library; her manuscripts are in the British Library, Department of Manuscripts (in the British Museum).

View from the bridge at Misterton Soss, photographed by Gwil Owen

Nottinghamshire

MISTERTON SOSS. On 28 September 1859 Lewes rowed George Eliot down from Gainsborough to the junction with the River Idle, 'which we ascended on foot some way, and walked back to Gainsborough'(Haight, p. 305). The first place they could have crossed the Idle, assuming they were following the north bank—which is where the road and the easier footpath run—is at Misterton Soss. At this place there are pumphouses on the parallel Mother Drain, easily identifiable by their two chimneys; they are now in ruins, and used as a kennels. According to Pevsner's *Buildings of England*, these pumphouses were 'built to house beam-engines (now gone) which propelled scoopwheels.' There must have been a good deal of machinery to see in George Eliot's day, and some of it would be both huge and wooden, as at the end of *The Mill on the Floss*. There is a plaque on the South building, which reads '1828 Alfred Smith Engineer'.

From the little bridge over the Mother Drain, the view resembles that of the first chapter of *The Mill on the Floss*; the houses along the Trent are approximately one mile away, and the low hills can be seen rising behind the alluvial plain. Immediately in front is the 'mill pond', in which the water was collected and directed to the wheels; behind is an overgrown plantation of withies. (There are even ducks disporting themselves and dogs barking, but I make no claim for their authenticity.)

Although she had written the 'early chapters' of *The Mill on the Floss* in May–June 1859, Gordon Haight's account of the manuscript in the New Clarendon edition (1980) makes it clear that the whole of the present Chapter 1 is a very late addition. This would support the case for the view from the bridge at Misterton Soss being the source for the view in the novel; we are told that George Eliot was well satisfied with her visit to Gainsborough because she had at last found the setting for her story.

NOTTINGHAM (Laceham)

Staffordshire (Loamshire in *Adam Bede*).

ELLASTONE (Hayslope). While a lot of ingenuity was misplaced in the nineteenth century in the attempt to identify the actual scenes of *Adam Bede* in the village, it is still a good place to visit in order to appreciate the general ambience.

One particular house in the village is associated with Robert Evans and his family and gives the impression of artisan wealth. Attempts to identify one or other of the various country houses— Wootton Hall, Calwich Abbey, Ilam Hall, Croxden Abbey—with the home of the Donnithornes are also made; it is of course the case that Robert Evans worked at Wootton Hall and was married at Ellastone Church.

ROCESTER (Rosseter).

Surrey

WITLEY, nr. Haslemere. The Heights was George Eliot's country house from 1877. It is now an old people's home.

Warwickshire (Loamshire in *Middlemarch* and *Felix Holt*).

ARBURY South Farm. George Eliot's birthplace.

ARBURY HALL —'the finest of all Early Gothic Revival houses in England' (Pevsner). Privately owned, it is open to visitors at certain times during the summer, usually Sundays and Bank Holidays. A guide book is available. As Cheverel Manor, it is the scene of 'Mr Gilfil's Love-Story'. For Robert Evans's work on the estate, see p. 13ff.

ARBURY MILL. The mill house has been altered since Mary Ann's youth, but there are stone steps where she is said to have sat, and a lawn. The mill itself has been much altered. It is an unusual mill in that it is first recorded in the eighteenth century, being part of Sir Roger Newdigate's canal system. Inside, the high breast-shot water-wheel can still be seen; it is 18 ft diameter and 4 ft wide. The various water-courses which fed the mill are no longer kept clear; the area of the mill is therefore quite muddy.

ASTLEY (Knebley). The church is described in 'Mr Gilfil's Love Story'. Well worth a visit to examine the medieval stalls, with their paintings of the Prophets and Apostles. Notice the memorial to Robert Evans's first wife, Harriet, 'for many years the friend and servant of the family at Arbury'. Robert also worked for the owners of Astley Castle nearby. Mrs Ann Garner, George Eliot's aunt lived at Sole End Farm.

CHILVERS COTON 'Shepperton Church' (see p. 88ff). Only the church tower survives from the nineteenth century. The church was bombed in the Second World War, and was rebuilt from 1946 to 1951; it has since been extended. Mary Ann Evans was christened here. In the churchyard are memorials to her parents, her brother Isaac and his family, and to Emma Gwyther ('Milly Barton').

Griff House is on the Coventry–Nuneaton Road. It is now a hotel. Much of it is unaltered, and it is usually possible to obtain permission to walk in the garden. Inside, the attics are always identified with those in *The Mill on the Floss*.

George Eliot's Coventry

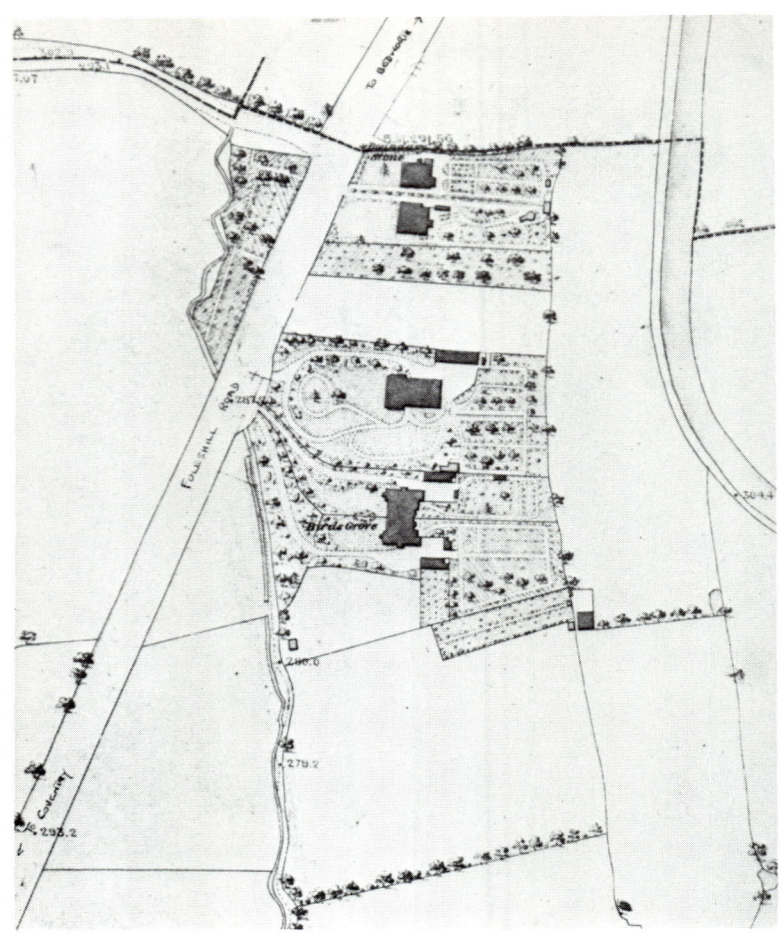

Large-scale plan of Bird Grove from the 1851 Ordnance Survey

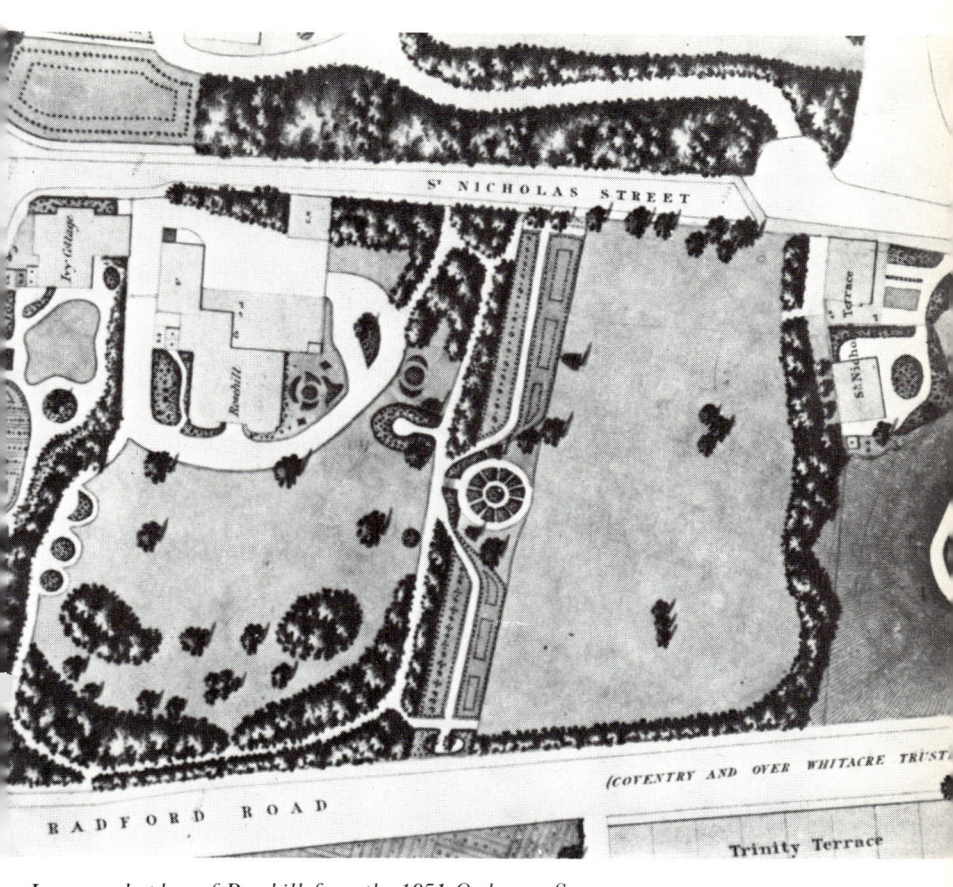

Large-scale plan of Rosehill from the 1851 Ordnance Survey

Griff Hollows ('The Red Deeps'), Gypsy Lane, and 'our brown canal' may easily be discovered in the surrounding area. In Chilvers Coton there is also to be seen the College for the Poor, really a kind of workhouse; it was constructed in 1800 by French prisoners of war. It features in 'Amos Barton'.

CORLEY. Corley Hall Farm is said to be Poyser's farm in *Adam Bede*.

COVENTRY (Middlemarch).

Three spires still dominate the skyline of the city, occasionally obscured by tower blocks. The new cathedral has risen next to the ruins of St Michael's Church, but Trinity Church, where Robert Evans worshipped, is still intact, though there have been Victorian restorations. Though the bombing of Coventry during the Second World War destroyed most of the city centre, the townplanners of the 1930s and the 1950s did away with most of the rest.

In the *Middlemarch* period the city was still quite restricted, as can be seen from the 1842 map, and George Eliot's school, her home at Bird Grove, and the Brays' house at Rosehill were all on the edges of the built-up area. In the early nineteenth century the town still depended on the ribbon trade, and on watch manufacture; the growth of the engineering industry came much later.

Nantglyn, 29 Warwick Row. This was the Misses Franklins' School; the house remains largely as it was from outside. Inside, it has been converted to house offices and a restaurant; the mock-tudor beams in the latter are misleading.

Bird Grove is a large semi-detached house in George Eliot Road, to the North of the town; it has been altered, and there are shops in the front garden.

Rosehill was at the top of the hill in St Nicholas Street, Radford.

The Herbert Art Gallery and Museum in Jordanwell has a small display of photographs and paintings connected with George Eliot and her circle; other items are on loan to the Nuneaton Museum.

In Broadgate House, Broadgate, the Coventry and Warwickshire Collection contains a comprehensive collection of books and pamphlets relating to George Eliot, besides being the principal local history library in the city.

FILLONGLEY—Isaac Pearson, George Eliot's uncle, was a farmer here; his tomb is in the churchyard of St Mary and All Saints.

GREAT PACKINGTON. Packington Hall is famous for its neo-Classical splendours, but remember that Robert Evans also worked on this estate for Lord Aylesford.

NUNEATON. George Eliot attended Mrs Wallington's Boarding School, which stood in Vicarage Street, formerly Church Lane; many early memories ought to be traceable in some way. The town is Milby in 'Janet's Repentance'. Unfortunately there has once again been bombing to contend with, and the town has been generous with George Eliot's name, which may cause confusion, e.g. there is a George Eliot Hospital. In the centre of the town you can see the George Eliot Hotel, formerly The Bull; the old name is visible on its façade. This was the Red Lion in 'Janet's Repentance'. Most of the other buildings in the story have gone, or been seriously altered; there are a number of relevant memorial tablets in the church and inscriptions in the churchyard.

The Museum, which stands in a little park, contains a large room devoted to George Eliot; there are some quite substantial souvenirs, e.g. her grand piano, and a large number of helpful pictures and documents. The Public Library also has a fine George Eliot collection.

Modern reminders of George Eliot abound, including the George Eliot Memorial Gardens, and the Dempster Coffee House.

STOCKINGFORD. Now a suburb of Nuneaton. St Paul's Church (1822–3) contains a memorial tablet to its second vicar, The Rev. J. E. Jones, who appears as Mr Tryan in 'Janet's Repentance'.

Yorkshire

LEEDS George Eliot visited Leeds in 1868 when *Middlemarch* was incubating. She stayed with a local Doctor who was opening a hospital; she wrote to Mme Bodichon on 25 September 'Our host Dr Allbutt is a good, clever, graceful man, enough to enable one to be cheerful under the horrible smoke of ugly Leeds: and the fine hospital, which he says, is admirably fitted . . .' The hospital is presumably the building at the end of Lyddon Terrace, which is now student flats. Nearby is Lyddon Hall, which is traditionally associated with this visit. The *Lyd* in *Lyd*gate is perhaps a half-conscious reminiscence.

Asia

There is a street named after George Eliot in Tel Aviv, Israel.

Europe

George Eliot made many visits abroad; one remembers how the valley of the Rhône, for example, appears in the text of *The Mill on the Floss*. In Germany she visited Cologne, Weimar, Munich, Berlin and Frankfurt. She made two visits to Florence while working on *Romola*, and travelled in Spain in conjunction with her poem *The Spanish Gypsy*. In Switzerland she spent a winter in

Geneva, staying first at the Campagne Plongeon, and then in the apartment of M. D'Albert Durade in the Rue des Chanoines; this is now the Rue de la Pélisserie.

Brief biographies

BELLOC, Bessie, Madame Louis Belloc, formerly Bessie Rayner Parkes (1829–95). Emancipated woman, wrote poetry and miscellaneous essays. She met George Eliot in 1852, and remained friends with her, supporting her decision to live with G. H. Lewes. She was the mother of Hilaire Belloc and Mrs Belloc Lowndes, who preserved certain oral traditions about George Eliot in her memoirs, entitled *I, too have lived in Arcadia*.

BLACKWOOD, John (1818–79). Member of the firm of William Blackwood and sons, Edinburgh publishers. He edited *Blackwood's Magazine* from 1845; G. H. Lewes contributed to it, and sent in George Eliot's first story. Blackwood published most of George Eliot's works, and remained a good friend, even though she once changed to another publisher.

BODICHON, Barbara, Madame Eugène, formerly Barbara Leigh Smith (1827–91). Painter. She was a cousin of Florence Nightingale, and a friend of Bessie Parkes (BELLOC). They met George Eliot together in 1852. She was a pioneer of women's education, and became one of the founders of Girton College. A constant correspondent, even when she became ill with hemiplegia, she was George Eliot's most sympathetic friend. In some ways she is connected with the character of Romola. Her life was written by Hester Burton.

BRABANT, Elizabeth Rebecca, called Rufa. Named by Coleridge because of her red hair. Daughter of Dr Brabant. She began the translation of Strauss which George Eliot completed. She married Charles Hennell, and later the Rev. W. M. W. Call.

BRABANT, Dr Robert Henry (1781–1866). Medical doctor, but became famous as a scholar, researching into Christian origins. He attracted George Eliot so much that she stayed with him at Devizes for a month in 1843: she was to be his 'second daughter', and read German and Greek with him. Mrs Brabant became jealous of this fervent discipleship and sent her away. This episode has been suggested as the germ of the Casaubon story (see Haight 50–1).

BRAY, Caroline, formerly Hennell (1814–1905). Unitarian. Wife of Charles, and sister of Charles and Sara Hennell. More conventional than her husband, she gave up writing to George Eliot from 1854 to 1859.

BRAY, Charles (1811–84). Ribbon manufacturer, phrenologist, author. Editor of the Coventry *Herald*, he was a town councillor of Coventry until the shopkeepers voted him off for helping to found the Co-op. His reminiscences of George Eliot are to be found in *Phases of Opinion and Experience during a Long Life: An Autobiography* (1885). New facts about his household have been discovered by Kathleen Adams—see her book, *Those of us who loved her* (1980).

CASAUBON, Isaac. A seventeenth century French scholar, born in Geneva. The correct pronunciation of the name, according to George Eliot, is Casaùburn. His life was written by Mark Pattison and was published in 1875; this led to a false identification of the character Casaubon with Pattison (see Haight).

CHAPMAN, John (1821–94). Publisher. He was two years younger than George Eliot, and came from Nottingham. He began his working life as a clockmaker's apprentice; after quarrelling with his master he ran away to Edinburgh, and then, hearing he was pursued, to Adelaide in South Australia, where he set up his own clock business. He returned to England and claimed to have trained as a doctor at Bart's; he finished this medical training at Paris in 1842, picking up some alarming ideas; luckily he was not qualified to practise surgery. In 1843 he married Susanna Brewitt, who was fourteen years older than himself; she inherited a considerable sum of money from her father in the ensuing year. Also in 1843 he bought the bookselling and publishing business of J. H. Green— an advanced Unitarian concern—and continued to run it on the same lines; therefore he was described to Emerson as 'a transcendental bookseller'. This is why he was the obvious publisher for George Eliot's translation of Strauss in 1846. For details of his affair with George Eliot see main text pp. 51–3. He continued to edit the *Westminster Review* until his death. For further information see Gordon S. Haight, *George Eliot and John Chapman: with Chapman's Diaries*, Archon Books (1969).

COMBE, George (1788–1858). Phrenologist. Disciple of Spurzheim. He founded the Phrenological Society, and the *Phrenological Journal*. He was a friend of Charles Bray. His voluminous correspondence with George Eliot is probably more important than is usually realised; her letters to him are published in the 1978 volumes.

COMTE, Auguste (1798–1857). Positivist thinker. Founder of the Religion of Humanity. One of the books which popularised his work was G. H. Lewes's *Comte's Philosophy of the Sciences*, and it is fair to assume that George Eliot helped him with the proofs *c.* 1853.

CROSS, John Walter (1840–1924). Banker. He married George Eliot in 1880. He had met the Leweses in 1869 and handled their financial affairs from 1872. His biography of George Eliot, compiled from her journals and letters, was carefully edited in the direction of respectability.

DURADE, François D'Albert (1804–86). Painter. George Eliot lived in his house in Geneva (1849–50). He translated five of her books into French.

EVANS, Elisabeth (Mrs Samuel), formerly Tomlinson (1776–1849). Late in life she wrote down her autobiography. It tells of her early employment as a lace-mender at Nottingham, and how at the age of twenty-one she was called to God's service. On Easter Tuesday, 1797, at a meeting at Beck Barn, she listened to the preaching of the Rev. George Smith. As the people saw the work of conversion they repeatedly broke into song, while sinners cried out for mercy. Elisabeth tells of her own conversion:

> 'I saw no confusion in the matter. I concluded that sinners were repenting of their sins, as I ought to do, and the people of God were so anxious for them to be saved, and these things caused them to rejoice. I longed for repentance more than ever I did for anything in my life, but I felt great hardness of heart. While I was looking to Christ the mighty power of God fell upon me in an instant. I fell to the ground like one dead. I believe I lost my senses for a season, but when I recovered I was trembling and weeping most bitterly. It pleased the Lord in about two hours to speak peace to my soul. I arose from my knees and praised God for that opportunity.

She joined the Methodists and gave up fashionable clothes and pastimes:

> I had entirely done with the pleasures of the world and with all my old companions. I saw it my duty to leave off all my superfluities in dress; hence, I pulled off all my bunches, cut off my curls, left off all my lace, and in this I found an unspeakable pleasure. I saw I could make a better use of my time and money than to follow the fashions of a vain world.

Instead she adopted a Quaker habit of dress. In March 1802 she was present at the last hours of Mary Voce (q.v.); in the summer of the same year she was appointed to preach at Ashbourne, and may at this time have preached in the open air at Ellastone. Samuel Evans saw her first at Ashbourne; she married him in the following year.

In 1803 the Wesleyan conference banned women preachers, but Elisabeth continued to find opportunities to use her abilities with the Primitive Methodists and the Derby Faith Folk. In her beliefs she was Arminian and did not share in the Calvinist gloom which later attracted Mary Anne Evans. After she married Samuel Evans she lived at Wirksworth in Derbyshire; she says of her marriage: 'The work of God broke out, and we had most powerful times.'

Elisabeth must be considered the original of Dinah Morris in two respects only: she told her niece the story of Mary Voce ('My Aunt's Story') in 1839, and she lived at a factory town (Snowhill) which is obviously Wirksworth. Otherwise there do not seem to have been any great resemblances between her and the character of Dinah.

EVANS, Isaac (1816–90). Brother of George Eliot. He succeeded their father as land-agent on the Arbury Hall estate. In certain respects the original of Tom Tulliver in *The Mill on the Floss*. Refused to communicate with his sister after hearing of her liaison with Lewes, but broke his silence to congratulate her on her marriage in 1880.

EVANS, Samuel (1777–1858). Uncle of George Eliot. Carpenter, later a manufacturer at Wirksworth. Methodist, being converted by a travelling preacher at the age of eighteen. Original of Seth Bede.

HENNELL, Charles (1809–50). Author of *An Inquiry Concerning the Origins of Christianity* (1838). Brother of Caroline Bray.

HENNELL, Sara (1812–99). Sister of above. She met George Eliot at Rosehill in 1842 and became her constant correspondent. She also wrote theological works of a diffuse nature which were the despair of her friends.

JAMES, Henry (1843–1916). Novelist. He wrote a vivid description of his first visit to George Eliot in 1869 (Haight, pp. 416–7). His reviews and articles about George Eliot are penetrating; his dialogue on *Daniel Deronda* is reprinted at the back of F. R. Leavis, *The Great Tradition*.

LEWES, George Henry (1817–78). See main text *passim*. For information about his family, see Haight.

LISZT, Franz (1811–86). Piano virtuoso and composer. In 1848 he became Musical Director to the Court at Weimar. George Eliot met him in Weimar in 1854, and was impressed by his kindness to her.

MYERS, F. W. H. (1843–1901). Poet, essayist and school inspector. A convinced spiritualist, he was one of the founders of the Society for Psychical Research. He invited George Eliot to Cambridge in May 1873.

PATTISON, Mark (1813–84). Rector of Lincoln College, Oxford. See CASAUBON

SIMCOX, Edith Jemima (1844–1901). Acolyte of George Eliot—whom she called 'Mother'. She left an account of her association with George Eliot in her unpublished *Autobiography of a Shirtmaker*. See K. A. McKenzie, *Edith Simcox and George Eliot*, Oxford (1961).

SPENCER, Herbert (1820–1903). Polymath. Slightly younger than George Eliot, Spencer was another Midlander, born in Derby. His family was Methodist, and he was drawn to Evangelicalism. His education had a mathematical and scientific bias, and he began work as a railway engineer. He found time to write, mainly articles about phrenology at first; he preserved its systematic approach to human behaviour. He taught himself geology, and decided that 'development' had taken place according to the theories of Lamarck: the wish to acquire characteristics had ultimately produced them, and the whole Universe exhibited a steady Progress towards higher forms of life. Spencer wished to systematise knowledge in relation to the laws of that Progress. His influence on the Victorians was immense; he became a sage. The many parallels with George Eliot show how suited they were to each other.

After a period of neglect, Spencer is now the subject of several books, which are more often concerned with his ideas than his life. See, for example, J. D. Y. Peel, *Herbert Spencer, the evolution of a sociologist*, Heinemann (1971).

VOCE, Mary (executed 16 March 1802). William Mottram, who was the great-nephew of Elisabeth Evans, gives the following details in *The True Story of George Eliot*. He is not always accurate, but may be presumed to have authority in the oral tradition of the family. Mary Voce was nineteen years old and was married to a bricklayer who deserted her; she poisoned her younger child and was condemned to death. Women preachers of the Methodist Church stayed in the jail with the murderess, and produced a last-minute conversion; another Methodist, John Clark, who was outside the jail, refused to eat or sleep until the woman was saved. The ballad of Mary Voce takes up the story:

> When Mary from the prison came,
>   A crowd had gathered round;
> But she was not dismayed, for now
>   Her heart true peace had found.
>
> Made happy in the love of God,
>   Calmly she took her leave;
> Jesus had eased her of her load,
>   She now disdained to grieve.

Her quickened soul so joyful was,
  So nerved by heavenly hope,
So eager for the awful change,
  She helped to fix the rope!

Nor did she dread the thought to die,
  When she was led away;
Her heavenly looks did testify
  It was a joyful day.

How eager were those pious souls,
  Who did on her attend,
To point her to the Lamb of God,
  The sinner's only Friend.

Ah, how they mourned for her distress
  With pity tried and true;
Their weak endeavours God did bless
  And owned their labours too.

All in a moment, as they prayed,
  Her rapt' rous voice exclaimed;
'O, what has Jesus done for me?
  My soul He has reclaimed.

He breaks my chains and sets me free,
  God does His love impart;
My load of guilt is gone, I feel
  The pardon on my heart.'

When to the fatal tree arrived,
  'Mary, we're here,' said one;
'Well, bless the Lord,' she then replied
  In a triumphant tone.

Then to the standers-by she said,
  'I pray you warning take;
Although I hang upon this tree,
  Jesus, my soul will take.'

And when the fatal cap was drawn,
  She must no longer stay:
'Glory, glory,' still she cried,
  And then was launched away.

All this was related to George Eliot by her aunt, and forms the germ of the Hetty Sorrel story in *Adam Bede*.

Further reading

The novels

After their first appearance in magazines or part-form, the novels were rapidly made available in volumes. Cheaper editions followed, and inevitably minor textual discrepancies began to occur. A complete edition of George Eliot's works, called the Cabinet edition, was put out in the late seventies and early eighties, to which Cross's biography was added after 1885. (A set of this edition was on offer in 1980 for £100).

At the time of writing the best set of novels is that provided in the Penguin English Library; it was completed for the centenary in 1980. All in all, the Penguin editions represent value for money, and have excellent introductions and annotation, together with bibliographical help. The later volumes are textually more rigorous than the earlier; a good deal of attention is now being paid to manuscript readings, and to the punctuation, which was not always George Eliot's own, but followed printers' conventions.

Oxford University Press have begun to publish the Clarendon editions, commencing with *The Mill on the Floss* (1980).

Letters

The sheer mass of the letters is daunting. Originally published in 1954-6 in seven volumes *The George Eliot Letters* were edited for Yale by Gordon S. Haight; two additional volumes have been added (1978). There is a copious index which is a joy to use. The quality of the letters, which were not written with an eye on publication, is very uneven, and they frequently deal with day-to-day topics. Nevertheless the early volumes, before she became famous, are a very good read.

Translation

The Essence of Christianity has been reprinted by Harper Torchbooks (1957).

Essays

At the moment these are out of print. Thomas Pinney, *Essays of George Eliot*, Routledge and Kegan Paul (1963) is to be preferred to any earlier collections, but it does not include *Impressions of Theo-*

phrastus Such; it does however give a full picture of her periodical criticism and other occasional writing of the 1850s.

Poems

There is no edition in print.

Notebooks

The 'Quarry for *Middlemarch*' was edited by A. T. Kitchel and published as a supplement to *Nineteenth Century Fiction* in 1950. *George Eliot: A Writer's Notebook 1854–1857* edited by Joseph Wiesenfarth is published by Virginia University Press (1981): it includes sketches of peasant-style hats for *Adam Bede*. See also *George Eliot's Blotter: A Commonplace-Book* edited for the British Library by Daniel Waley (1980) which is on sale in the British Museum.

Biography

The standard biography is that of G.S. Haight, Oxford University Press (1968); it is simply called *George Eliot: A Biography*. Readers' responses to this vary a good deal; some find it a fascinating read, but others are overwhelmed by the amount of factual material. A better introduction might be provided by Marghanita Laski, *George Eliot and her World*, Thames and Hudson (1973); this occasionally supplies information not in Haight, and has an excellent selection of pictures—but on the other hand Laski does tend to play up the reactions of some of George Eliot's more hostile contemporaries.

Of the many earlier biographies John Walter Cross, *George Eliot's Life as related in her Letters and Journals* (1885) was the official biography, but it has the faults of the genre; it seems to have had the approval of her brother Isaac, and, as Haight has shown, its texts of the letters are not to be trusted. There are some other early lives, such as Mathilde Blind, *George Eliot* (1883) and Oscar Browning, *George Eliot* (1890), which now have a special value as the records of those who knew her.

Kathleen Adams, *Those of us who loved her*, The George Eliot Fellowship (1980) contains new information about George Eliot's immediate circle.

Curiosities

A number of very strange productions, mainly hagiographical, can sometimes be found in second-hand bookshops. In her own lifetime George Eliot, presumably persuaded by Lewes, allowed Alexander Main to issue *Wise, Witty and Tender Sayings of George Eliot* (1871);

this regard for the 'wisdom' of the novelist is, as Isobel Armstrong has pointed out, a way of reading the text which we have lost. Main followed his success with *The George Eliot Birthday Book* (1878). There are also early books which attempt to give a record of scenes associated with George Eliot in watercolours or photographs, e.g.
Emily Swinnerton (ed.), *George Eliot: her early home* (1893)
William Mottram, *The True Story of George Eliot* (1905)
Such books help us to visualise the nineteenth-century appearance of the buildings and the countryside; they also provide unwitting testimony to the tastes and interests of her first readers.

Criticism

Most of the older books on George Eliot's novels have now been superseded. Virginia Woolf wrote a long essay on the occasion of the centenary (1919), which is reprinted in *The Common Reader* and in her *Collected Essays*; but modern criticism of George Eliot really begins with two books published in 1948 by Cambridge lecturers, marking the great respect given to the novels in university studies:
Joan Bennett, *George Eliot: her Mind and Art*, Cambridge University Press
F. R. Leavis, *The Great Tradition*, Chatto and Windus.
Leavis's book was based on articles written much earlier, and has subsequently been revised. In the nineteen-fifties there was considerable emphasis on form in the novel, and the recent discoveries of Shakespearean critics were applied to the text of George Eliot. The foremost of all the critical books of this school is Barbara Hardy's *The Novels of George Eliot: A Study in Form*, Athlone Press (1959) which must be read for its study of imagery and patterns to be found within the text. In the nineteen-sixties W. J. Harvey, *The Art of George Eliot*, Chatto and Windus (1961) is especially valuable for its study of the structure of the novels.

With the deepening of interest in individual novels in recent years, critics have been less inclined to write general studies, and a great deal of work has gone on in journals and periodicals exploring particular areas. This has led to the assembly of several fine collective works. For material from the nineteenth and twentieth centuries see:
G. S. Haight, *A Century of George Eliot Criticism*, Methuen (1965)
David Carroll, *George Eliot: The Critical Heritage*, Routledge and Kegan Paul (1971).
Barbara Hardy has edited two collections: *Middlemarch*, Athlone (1967) and *Critical Essays on George Eliot*, Routledge and Kegan Paul (1970). A number of other books and articles offer critical insights but are more concerned with special areas of interest. These are listed next.

ART Hugh Witemeyer, *George Eliot and the Visual Arts*, Yale (1979)

HISTORICAL BACKGROUND TO 'MIDDLEMARCH' John Prest, *The Industrial Revolution in Coventry*, Oxford University Press (1960)
Jerome Beaty, 'History by Indirection:the Era of Reform in *Middlemarch*' in *Victorian Studies* (1957)

'ROMOLA' AS A HISTORICAL NOVEL Andrew Sanders, *The Victorian Historical Novel 1840–1880*, Macmillan (1979)

RELIGION Most general studies of Victorian religion are concerned with doctrine or give an overview from above. In a book with a totally different approach, working from the ground up, James Obelkevich has carefully analysed what actually happened in one small area. His *Religion and Rural Society: South Lindsey 1825–1875*, Oxford University Press (1976) confirms many of George Eliot's sociological observations, particularly about the new assertiveness of the Church of England in this period. His references to 'pagan' survivals, too, are fascinating, considering that the Dodsons are placed in rural Lincolnshire.

RELIGIOUS NOVELS, RELIGION IN NOVELS Robert Lee Woolf, *Gains and Losses*, John Murray (1977)
Valentine Cunningham, *Everywhere Spoken against: Dissent in the Victorian Novel*, Oxford University Press (1975)
U. S. Knoepflmacher, *Religious Humanism in the Victorian Novel*, Princeton (1965)

GEORGE ELIOT'S OWN IDEAS AND BELIEFS George Willis Cooke, *George Eliot: A Critical Study of her Life, Writings and Philosophy* (1883). A pioneer study, long out of print, makes it quite clear what ideas were present to Victorian intellectuals; the book stresses her Positivism and her appeal as a rationalist. While praising the 'nobility' of her ideas it is curiously free from the hankering after a 'Christian really all the time' version of George Eliot which characterises many books written after the Second World War. For Cooke there is nothing sad about the fact that George Eliot lost her faith; the old religion is quite dead, and George Eliot is a herald of the future. All modern studies of her beliefs are indebted to Basil Willey, *Nineteenth Century Studies*, Chatto and Windus (1949); the whole should be read, not just the chapters devoted to George Eliot. The stress is quite the opposite of Cooke's, as indicated above. A nice short essay is 'Qualities of George Eliot's Unbelief' in Humphry House, *All in Due Time*, Rupert Hart-Davis (1955). More difficult is Bernard Paris, *Experiments in Life: George Eliot's Quest for Values*, Wayne, Detroit (1965), which claims to be the first book about George Eliot's ideas since Cooke. And see *Darwin's Plots* by Gillian Beer, Routledge and Kegan Paul (1983) for an account of Darwin's influence on Victorian novelists: there are chapters on *Middlemarch* and *Daniel Deronda*.

REALISM Richard Stang, *The Theory of the Novel in England 1850–1870*, Routledge and Kegan Paul (1959)
U. S. Knoepflmacher, *George Eliot's Early Novels: the limits of Realism*, University of California Press (1968).

For the more recent debate on *Middlemarch* as 'the Classic Realist text' see the first chapter of Colin McCabe, *James Joyce and the Revolution of the World*, Macmillan (1978); this is answered by David Lodge in '*Middlemarch* and the idea of the Classic Realist Text', an essay to be found in Arnold Kettle (ed.) *The Nineteenth Century Novel*, Heinemann Educational Books/Open University Press (1981).

Influence of George Eliot on other writers

THE MILL ON THE FLOSS was of supreme importance to Proust— 'Two pages . . . can bring tears to my eyes'. In English literature the line descends through Hardy to D. H. Lawrence, whose first novel, *The White Peacock*, illustrates how a writer learns by imitation, in this case of *Adam Bede*; see especially the chapter 'A Shadow in Spring'. For George Eliot's influence on Henry James, see F. R. Leavis, *The Great Tradition*.

Appendix

Some letters from Robert and Isaac Evans

These letters are a tiny selection from those written by Robert Evans to his employer. They show 'Caleb Garth' at his activities, and the last letter has an accompanying pencil 'plan of a cottage' which must illuminate the philanthropic schemes of Dorothea. All this helps to indicate the rich compost of real life from which *Middlemarch* grew. The letter about the fire is unusual; and no reference to a fire at Griff has been previously noted. Mary Ann was not present, of course, on this occasion. The third letter shows Isaac taking command, like Tom Tulliver, at a time of crisis, and the fourth letter refers to the death of Mrs Gwyther, which is the germ of the story of 'Amos Barton'.

To: F. Newdigate Esqre
      Dartmouth House
      Black Heath
      London

Griff March 3rd 1833

Sir,
I received your letters at Packington on Thursday last—the Tenant which I was in hopes would take Tafts Farm was Mr Proof of Corley Lord Liffords Tenant, but I am sorry to say that he will not take it, the land that Lagon pretended to fallow will want fallowing again this year, the Yard at home not stoned, the New road from the Corley Road not yet compleated, that it frightens all the Tenants away that come to look at it, and also this very wet season is very much against the letting of a cold Farm, we have nearly finished with all the soughing in the Great riddings but it has been a terable job to get the tiles to it. It is now my opinion that it will not be let this year to any responsable Tenant, we must therefore keep a team and Implements to work the Farm ourselves and get it in as good order as possable against the next Lady day 1834 and sell the remainder at the Dukes Farm, and it is about time now to fix on the day of Sale, and I think Tuesday, Wednesday or Thursday the 19th–20th or 21st or this month will do. I intend looking out the Horses, Implements and some sticks to keep for Tafts Farm, and have the Auctioneer to make an Inventory of the

184

remainder of the Stock (-?) on Tuesday next, and I shall be much obliged if you will write to me to Packing [ton?] on Thursday next. I shall always make a point of being at Packington on a Thursday and till noon on Friday or to be at home always on a Saturday Except Accidents, you will Please to give me any Advice or Directions you think Proper—I have seen Mr. Stratton and he tells me you intend being here about the 14th. I think I can be at home or about home, from the 14th to the 18th if you can make it convenient to be here on any of those days. I shall be glad to see you, as I wish to have many things settled for future arrangements.

I must now enter upon a very painful subject that is concerning Henry Ball, I settled with him on the 26th Jan: last as soon as I had make up m[y]last ye[ar's] accounts with Lord Aylesford, and I [-?paid] him up to the end of Jan: and then give him [a] quarters Salary instead of giving him notice to leave before the accounts were made up, after all this he was above one hundred in my Debt.—he had received the day before £65 therefore I left him to pay all the men up to the end of Jan: and make out the Farming accs^{ts} for Ld Aylesford against I went to Packington on Thursday on 12th Feb:—I went on that day and he had gone away that morning before I arrived there, and he had paid some of the things that I ordered him, he had taken the Books with him which he was deficient in, and I was Obliged to pay the men according to their demand—while I was writing this a Mr Dickin from Meriden has just come to me at Griff to ask me for £50 that Mr Ball had borrowed in Ld Aylesford's name and mine which I suppose I must pay, I have found him a very dishonest man. I do not know where my loss will end—he sold all his things [to?] a Mr Ball of Coleshill and he fetched them away from Packington unknown to me and pretended they were to be directed to New Yoark but I consider him to be some w[h]ere in the Nighbourhood, and that his friend Mr Ball knows where he is. I have never seen him since 26th Jan: when I gave him notice that I could not keep him any longer and I expected he had wrote to his Friends till last Thursday. Ld Aylesford said he had several letters for him and wanted to know where he c^d send them to please to let Lady Dartmouth and his parents know and they will say where the letters may be sent to.

      I am Sir. Y^r most Obt
      Hum^{le} Sev^t
          R. Evans (signature)

To F Newdigate Esqre
　　Black Heath
　　London

Griff December 16th 1833

Sir,
I received your very kind letter which I feal most gratefull for. Mrs Evans kept up her Spirits wonderfull while the fire lasted, and that was the case with myself, for I had the presents of mind to Act and direct in every point w[h]ere there was the most danger, and my courage never failed me during the day and night, but Mrs Evans and myself since that time have had but little sleep. Still we feal very thankfull that the House and Buildings are saved, but that was with the greatest Exertion that we kept the fire back as the cowshed was on fire many times, and the men that stud upon it, as I saw all the nine ricks were condem^d I fixed all the forces of Engins and men between the Ricks and the Buildings, for if the cowshed which is thatched had fired so as to get master of us every Building must have been burnt to the Ground the fire first caught the waggon Hovel which is 60ft long, and the roof raised from the Bearers with kids and thatched the men on the coalpit saw it begin the Size of your hand and if they had Immediately helped a man on the roof with a shovel it might have been stoped by beating it down—I was at Coton Industry when the fire broke out, they sent a Horse for me and I was at home in a quarter of an hour after it began, and every Stack was in flame.

　I had sent from Coton for the Nuneaton Engine so it was very soon after me and put to work at the rick next the cowshed. Mr Law's Engine was there the first and with that and the Nuneaton Engine and some Hundred of men and Buckets we checked it from the Buildings till 3 Engines arrived from Coventry, but by this time the flames of all the stacks at once produced such a heat that for 2 hours we allmost dispaired of saving the cowshed. When I tell you the Heat was such that you could not bear your hand on the barn doors. Then I had all the Straw and Grain carried out of the Barn and Granary and taken to a Distance out of the wind so as the Sparks w^d not follow it, and at this time fire got into the Granary through the tiling and set fire to some paper Bags with seeds in them—the fire began ab^t 12 at noon and I think it was 8 or 9 before we were in a state to consider the Buildings safe, then we directed the Engines to play upon one Stack bottom at a time, till most of the fire was out and so continued from one to another till all were put out which was 12 o'clock midnight when the Engines left, but still there were fire left smoking in all the bottoms of the stacks—Mr Buchanan was here who is the Agent to the

Insurance and he ordered 50 men to stop on the Ground allnight, to attend to the fire and keep any Bad people from doing mischief

He directed me to make a Valuation of all the ricks and Farming Implements which I did the next day and took it to his Office yesterday and swore to it, the amount of the Valuation is 840–16–0 besides the waggon Hovel and Other things which are not Insured. I am sorry to say that I have only Insured to the Amount of 400 not thinking that I had nearly 2 years crop in the Backyard—I never had so good Stackyard in all my life and every handfull of Wheat, Oats, Clover and Hay was got so well the loss is very Great besides the trouble and disappointment for the time to come the whole loss of Stacks, Buildings, Implements and other things can not be laid at less that £1000nd—and the whole of this has been caused by the mismanagement of the Ground Bailieff, and the Agent of the Colliery before you had it on a lease—I spoke to Davenport before any pit had ever began in that [?close] and also to Mr Stratton, but several times to Davenport—John Larrance can attest—and desired him to measure the length of the ground that the coals lay under from the bottom of my field against the Garden to the Houses in Griff telling at the same time that the coal might be got with 2 pits but I perceived they w^d do as they liked so I told them they might put w[h]ere they pleased therefore they put it in the worst place the[y] possibly could—the swar has always [illegible] which I pointed out which w^d have saved the Stackyard.

                I am Sir. your most O^{bt} Servt.

                          R. Evans

[Isaac writes as his father is ill
— on black edged paper because his mother has died]

To: F. Newdigate Esq
      Dartmouth House
      Black Heath
      Kent

Griff Feby 15th 1836

Sir,
I have arranged with Snow about going to London, he has taken his place by the Greyhound Coach which leaves Coventry on Wednesday night and arrives at the Swan with two necks, Lad Lane, on Thursday morning about 7 o'clock, and I have requested him to wait there until he finds the person to conduct him to Black heath.—I am happy to say my Father has been gradually gaining strength ever since the change in his disease notwithstanding the loss of my Mother, which is a source of much grief to all of us— I take the liberty of informing you that my Father has put a value on the Arbury Estate and the Tenants signed their Agreements on Saturday last and seemed very well satisfied with the Rents which they have to pay on Thursday next.

   My father wished me to say that there is some Ash and Elm timber on W. Swinnerton's and Thos Garner's Farms which he thinks should be taken down if you have no objection to it. Richard Shaw is sent by Astley Parish to a Lunatic Assylum and his wife and family are to leave at Lady Day and Jephcote the under Keeper at Arbury is to have the House which will be entered in the Arbury Rental for the future

                I am Sir
              Your most ob^t hum^{ble} Ser^t

Isaac P. Evans.

To F Newdigate (as before)

Griff Nov 10th 1836

Sir,
I write to desire you to fix the Hallam Rent day, I find that I have a great deal to do in the month of December, therefore I must calculate my time as well as I can, I have several things to fix, but till you have determined the week that you wish me to be at Hallam I cannot arange my work, if Monday the 12th of Dec^b to Sunday the 18th will sute you it will do very well for me, as that was the week that the rent day was held last Dec^b but you will Please to make out your own Plan and I shall be much Obliged if you will write to me to meet me at Packington on Wedensday morning next, under cover to Lord Aylesford as I shall be at Packington that morning by 10 o'clock, and only stop that day as I must attend a meeting at Corley on the Tithe Commutation Act on Thursday next, but I do not expect Mr Gregory and the Land Owners will agree without a Valuation, as they have been paying a high tithe from 1824 something like the Kirk Hallam, I suppose you will have Some (?) Difficulty in settling with *Mr Wilkinson* tho West Hallam will be very little trouble

I am glad to see the price of Corn Improved so that the Farmers will be able to pay their Rents better than they have done for some years back, Wheat is likely to be very high towards next Spring as the Turnips are a failing Crop this year, and the Hay Crop about half a Crop, I hope for a Mild Winter or else I do not know what Farmers will do with their Store (?) Stock—I am sorry to tell you that poor Mrs Gwyther will be Buried tomorrow—She was confined about 3 weeks back and never recovered—the child is alive and well and likely to live, She has left 7 small children, I am very sorry for Mr Gwyther I do not know what he will do with such a family and so small an income,

      I am Sir,
      Your most O^{bt}
      Hum^{le} Servt
        R Evans.

To F Newdigate etc

Griff July 8th 1839

Sir,
I received your Astley Rents on the 1st of this month and on Friday last I paid to your account at Little and Woodcocks Bank Coventry £*635* I have been this day to the Marylands to Plan the Cottage and buildings and to set the men to pull down the old Ruins of the Cottage and Barn, I shall send you a scetch of my Plan on the otherside. I must keep it on as Small a Scale as I can, as it is a very small Farm, it is mearly a cottage with a Pantry or Small dairy and 2 Chambers a small Barn and a little Cowshed which I hope you will approve of, after this is done I hope I shall not want to spend any more upon the Buildings on your Astley Estate—except Materials to the Tenants for common repairs, The last week was very Hot I was walking over the Great Packington Estate and it nearly nocked me up, and have been unwell since, but am now getting well I hope—I hope your son was pleased with his journey into Derbyshire and that the country answered his expectations, and that you returned home to Black Heath quite safe and well.

$$\text{I am Sir,}$$
$$\text{Your most O}^{bt}$$
$$\text{Hum}^b \text{ S erv}^t$$
$$\text{R. Evans}$$

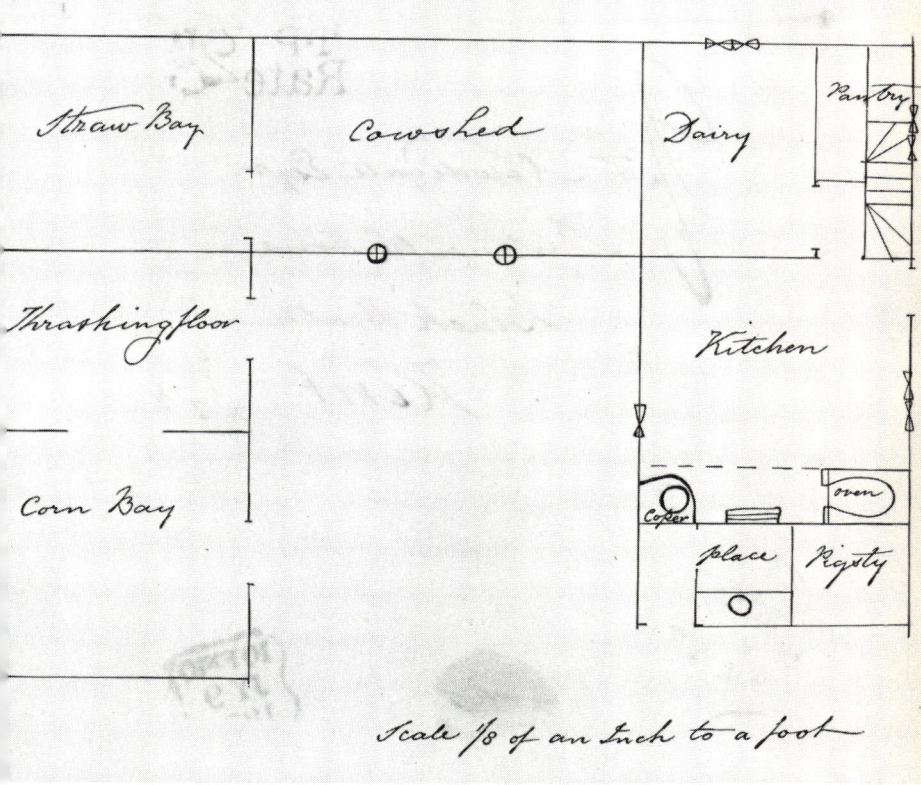

Plan of a cottage by Robert Evans, redrawn from an original pencil-sketch

Acknowledgements

I should like to thank Ted Holt for help with Feuerbach, and Nora Tomlinson for reading a draft of the manuscript; the music section is largely the work of the General Editor, Maurice Hussey, who has been generous with time and encouragement throughout the preparation of the book. A grant from the Arts Faculty Research Fund of the Open University enabled me to visit many of the places associated with George Eliot. Mrs Kathleen Adams of the George Eliot Fellowship helped me over many points of detail, and I should like to thank the Fellowship for permission to quote from Robert Evans's diaries. Robert Evans's letters are quoted by kind permission of F. H. M. FitzRoy Newdegate Esq. and the Warwickshire County Record Office.

The author and publishers are grateful to the following for permission to reproduce photographs and original artwork:
BBC Hulton Picture Library, page 71; Borghese Gallery, Rome, page 100 (photo Giraudon); British Library, pages 99 and 138; Coventry and Warwickshire Reference Library, pages 166–9; Herbert Art Gallery, Coventry, pages 12 and 120; Homerton College, Cambridge, pages 110–11; Illustrated London News Picture Library, page 89; Manchester City Art Gallery, page 84; Mansell Collection, page 112; Mary Evans Picture Library, page 35; National Gallery, page 63; National Portrait Gallery, pages ii, 50 and 56; Nottingham Local History Library, page 127; Tate Gallery, page 61; Thorvaldsens Museum, Copenhagen, page 40; Warwickshire County Records Office, page 191; Reproduced by Gracious Permission of Her Majesty the Queen, page 32.
The photograph on page 163 was taken by Gwil Owen.

The painting *Coventry* by J. M. W. Turner is reproduced on the cover by permission of the Department of Prints and Drawings, British Museum.

General index

à Kempis, Thomas, 31, 70, 105, 119, 132
Acton, Lord, 58
Allbutt, Dr 171
American Civil War, 152
Antigone, 150
Arbury Farm, 13, 165
Arbury Hall, 13, 16, 21, 22, 165
Arbury Mill, 165
Ariadne, 144
Arnold, Matthew, 66
Astley, 14, 29, 165
Austen, Jane, 92, 95
Aylesford, Lord, 13, 170

Bedworth, 16
Bellini, 74
Belloc, Bessie, 173
Bennett, Arnold, 153
Bird Grove, 23, 168, 170
Birmingham, 18, 20, 31
Blackwood, John, 60, 67–8, 70, 76, 92, 95, 96, 101, 173
Blackwood's Magazine, 53, 68, 92–3
Bodichon, Barbara, 65, 79, 171, 173
Brabant, Dr, 173
Brabant, Rufa, 39, 173
Bray, Caroline (Hennell), 23–4, 34, 39, 173
Bray, Charles, 23–4, 34, 36–7, 49, 51, 52, 170, 174
Broadstairs, 54
Bronte(s), 21, Charlotte, 38, 55, 69
Browning, Oscar, 72, 180

Cambridge, 79, 161
Carlyle, Thomas, 109
Casaubon, Isaac, 174
Catholic Emancipation, 28
Cervantes, 59
Chambers, Robert, 36
Chapman, John, 41, 51–4, 57, 174
Chilvers Coton, 13, 16, 29, 93, 165, 170
Chilvers Coton church, 15, 88–91, 165, 170
cholera, 16
Christ in the house of his parents, 61
'Christ-image', 39–40
Church of England, 20, 27–31, 117, 182
church-restoration, 88–91

Clough, Arthur Hugh, 41–2
Coleridge, S. T., 39
Combe, George, 37, 174
Communion Service, 43–4
Comte, Auguste, 45–7, 57, 79, 85, 132, 174
Cokke, George Willis, 182
cottages, building, 15, 190–1
Coventry, 13, 16, 18, 20, 23, 31, 52, 73, 134, 166–9, 170, 174
Craik, Mrs, 69
Cross, J. W., 68, 76; 174–5, 180
Cumming, Dr, 30, 78

D'Albert Durade, François, 49–51, 78–80, 172, 175
de Beauvoir, Simone, 105
Derbyshire, 11, 14, 18, 161
determinism, 36, 38, 152, 154
Deutsch, Emanuel, 155
Dickens, Charles, 62, 133
Docker, Mr, 15, 20, 31
Dutch painting, 18, 60, 62–4

Ebdell, Bernard Gilpin, Rev., 29
Economist, The, 54, 74

ELIOT, GEORGE (Mary Ann Evans)
her names at different times, 2, 51, 67–9
born, 13
baptism, 29, 165
education, 15, 19–22
moves to Coventry, 16, 23
attitude to manual labour, 17–18
writing practice, 18–19
housekeeper at Griff, 21–2
social conscience, 22
read poetry, 22–3
loss of faith, 24–6, 34
religious development, 24–48
'Holy War', 24–6
phrenological diagnosis, 37
translations, 39–45
Positivist (Comtist) views, 45–8, 75
in Geneva, 49–51
new life style, 51

stays at Chapman's, 51–7
union with Lewes, 44, 57–8
begins to write fiction, 59–66
life at the Priory, 70–2
political views, 19, 72–3, 85, 87, 90–1
musical interests, 73–6
marriage to Cross, 76
death, funeral, grave, 34, 76–8, 162
Eliot, T. S., 95
Ellastone, 11, 159, 164–5
Emerson, 22, 51, 174
Evangelicalism, 20–4, 27–31, 34, 36, 46, 59, 78, 93–5, 113, 132
Evans, Christiana (Chrissey), 13–4, 19, 22
Christiana (Pearson), Mrs, 13–22, 186, 188
Elizabeth (Tomlinson), Mrs Samuel, 31, 96, 159, 161, 175–6
Fanny, 76
Isaac, 13–5, 17, 19–21, 25, 76, 107, 165, 176, 188
Mary Anne (Marian) see GEORGE ELIOT
Robert, 11–26, 31, 64, 108, 159, 161, 164–5, 170, 184–91
journal, 14–16, 24, 26
Robert (jnr.), 14
Samuel, 31, 159, 161, 175–6

Feuerbach, Ludwig, 42–6, 58, 64, 68, 80, 97, 107
Florence, 65, 108–115
Fortnightly, 69
Frankfurt, 155, 171
Franklin, Francis, Rev. 20, 25
Franklin, Misses, school 20, 31, 170
Frazer, Sir James, 144
French Revolution, 28

Gainsborough, 162, 164
Gall, F. J. 36
Geneva, 49–51, 170
German scholarship *see* 'Higher criticism'
Germany, 57–8, 83–5
Girton College, 161, 173

193

Goethe, 58
Goldsmith, Oliver, 92
Gospels, 39–41
Gothic Revival, 13, 65, 165
Great Packington, 13, 25, 165
Greek tragedy, 121
Griff, 13, 18, 21, 165, 184
Gwyther, Mr, 15, 93, 189
   Mrs Emma, 165, 184, 189
gypsies, 155

Hardy, Barbara, 152, 181
Hegel, 42
Hennell, Caroline *see* Bray
   Charles, 23–4, 39, 42, 176
   Sara, 34, 39, 176
'Higher criticism' of the Bible, 24, 39–45
Highgate Cemetery, 76–8, 162
Hireling Shepherd, The, 62, 83–4
Holman Hunt, 62, 83–4
humanity, religion of, 42–8, 64, 79, 97, 149
Hunt, Thornton, 57

Idle, River, 162–4
Ilfracombe, 58
Imitation of Christ, The, *see* à Kempis
Israel, 171

James, Henry, 18, 150, 176
Jervis, Agnes, 57–8, 72, 144
Jones, Mr Edmund, 30, 171
Jones, Owen, 70
Judaism, 155–6

Keats, 149
Kirk Hallam, 11
Kirkby, 14

Lamb, Charles, 91
Lawrence, D. H., 104, 153, 183
Leader, 43
Leavis, F. R., 119, 150, 181
Leeds, 171
Lewes, Agnes, *see* Jervis
Lewes, Charles, 78
Lewes, G. H. 2, 37, 44, 46, 55–9, 67–72, 74, 76–7, 80, 91–2, 107–8, 114, 121, 144, 156, 162
Lewis, Miss Maria, 20–1, 23, 24, 30, 59
Liggins, 68
Lincolnshire, 162
Linton, Eliza Lynn, 57
Liszt, 74–5, 176

Locke, John, 156
London, 51–4, 70–2, 76–7, 126, 162
Lyrical Ballads, 66–7, 93, 96

Mackay, William, 51
Main, Alexander, 180
marriage as 'free union', 44
Martineau, Harriet, 46
Marx, Karl, 42
Massey, Bartle, 11, 20 *and see Adam Bede*
Mendelssohn, 74
Meredith, George, 55
Methodism, 28, 31–3, 96, 161, 175–7
Mill, James, 53
Mill, John Stuart, 53, 66
Millais, 61–2
Misterton Soss, 162–4
Morris, William, 64
Mulock, Miss, 69
music, 30, 73–6
Myers, F. W. H., x, 79–80, 176
mythology, 41, 51, 144

Newdigate, Francis (Parker), 11–16, 184ff
Newdigate, Sir Robert, 11–13, 165
Newman, John Henry, 28
News from Nowhere, 64
Nonconformism, 20–1, 31–4, 122
Norbury, 161
Nottingham, 164, 174–5
Nuneaton, 15, 20, 24, 29–30, 95, 121, 170–1

opera, 74
oratorios, 30, 74
'originals', 159
Oxford Movement, 28, 30–1

Pantheism, 23, 80
Parker, Francis, *see* Newdigate
Pattison, Mark, 177
Peacock, Thomas Love, 36
Pearson, Christiana, *see* Mrs Evans
Pearson, Isaac, 16, 170
peasantry, 83, 119, 121
Peel, 90, 123–5
phrenology, 23, 34–8, 46
Positivism, 45–7, 75, 80, 113, 115, 131–2, 150, 156
Poynton, Harriet, 11, 165
Pre-Raphaelitism, 62, 64–5
Prest, John, 134–5
Priory, The, 70–2, 76, 162

Proust, 183

Radicals, 122–3
Realism, 18, 43, 59–64, 92–3, 101, 107, 150, 153, 156, 182–3
Reform, 53–73, 122, 125
Reform Bill (1832), 28, 121, 123–5
Reform Bill (1867), 73, 121
religious novels, 92, 182
Rembrandt, 60, 62
Rosehill, 169, 170
Rossetti, 64
Roston Common, 11
Rubinstein, Anton, 75
Ruskin, 60, 62, 86–7

St Theresa, *see* Theresa
Sand, George, 69
Savonarola, 108–115, 131–2
Scott, Sir Walter, 21, 59, 83, 108
Shakespeare, 156
Shelley, 57
Simcox, Edith, 77–8, 177
Simeon, Charles, 28
Simms, Edward, 73
social science, 54–5, 83–4, 118
Spain, 131, 171
Spencer, Herbert, 36, 53–5, 57, 68, 74, 85, 87, 119, 144, 176
spiritualism, 80
Spurzheim, 36
Staffordshire, 11, 18, 164–5
Stockingford, 18, 171
Strauss, David Friedrich, 39–43, 51, 58, 66

Taylor, Isaac, 23, 80
Tempest, The, 74, 156
Tenby, 58
Tennyson, Alfred, 28
Thackeray, Anny, 72, 77
Theresa, St. 130–2, 144, 149–50
Tilley, Elisabeth, 52
Tomlinson, Elizabeth, *see* Evans
Trollope, Anthony, 92

Unitarians, 23, 33–4, 174

Venice, 76
Victoria, Queen, 101
von Riehl, Wilhelm Heinrich, 21, 83–8, 90–1, 93, 101, 119, 121

Wallace, A. R. 36

Wallington, Mrs, 15, 20, 170
Warwickshire, 11–26, 87, 121, 126, 165–71
Weimar, 58
Wesley, John, 31
Westminster Abbey, 58, 162

Westminster Review, 34, 37, 53, 57, 83, 174
Wilberforce, William, 28, 60
Willey, Basil, 27, 182
Wirksworth, 161, 176
Witley, 76, 165
Woolf, Virginia, 150, 181
Wootton Hall, 11, 164

Wordsworth, 22, 46–7, 59, 65–7, 78, 87–8, 93–4, 105, 142

Yonge, Charlotte, 31
Yorkshire, 171
Young, Edward, 78

Index to George Eliot's works and literary topics

NB: characters are referred to by first name or surname as normally used in the novels. Main references are in italics.

Adam Bede, x, 11, 17–8, 29, 31–3, 38, 42–5, 47, 62–3, 66–9, 74, 85, 88, 91, 95, *96–104*, 119, 159, 161, 164–5, 170, 176–8
Adam Bede, 17–8, 43–4, 96–7, 101
'Address to Working Men', 73
'Amos Barton, The Sad Fortunes of the Rev.', 15, 19, 31, 60, 67–8, 78, *88–98*, 165, 170, 184
Arthur Donnithorne, 38, 101–4
author's reservations, 129, 139, 148, 156
autobiographical references, 167–8

Baldassarre, 108–9
Bartle Massey, 11, 44
Brooke, Mr, 124, 126, 134–6
'Brother and Sister' sonnets, 19
Bulstrode, 30, 33, 135, 146–8
Bulstrode, Mrs Harriet, 137, 146–7
Burning of the Vanities, The, 110–11

Cabinet edition, 179
Cadwallader, Mrs, 135, 143–4
Caleb Garth, 11–18, 149, 184 ff
Casaubon, 39, 51, 114, 125–6, 135, 143–5, 173
Celia, 139–42
character-creation, 143–9, 154
Chettam, Sir James, 126, 135, 143, 146
childhood, 67

Daniel Deronda, xi, 64, 69–70, 74–5, 78, 80, *151–6*, 176, 183
Daniel Deronda, 146, 152–6

Dinah Morris, 32–3, 47, 96–101, 159
Dodsons, 13–4, 16, 88, 106, 116–8, 182
Dorothea, 22, 30, 44, 73, 108, 114–5, 125–7, 131–2, 134, 139–46, 149, 184

Ecclesiastical History, chart of, 23
epigraphs, 153–4
Essence of Christianity, The, 42–5, 179, *and see* Feuerbach in General Index
Esther Lyon, 121–3, 125–6
'Evangelical Teaching', 30
experimental writing, 152–6

Farebrother, Mr, 29–30, 143, 147–8
Featherstone, 119, 133, 135, 146
Felix Holt, 38, 65, 73, 88, 114, *121–3*, 125, *128–9*
Felix Holt, 38, 122–3, 128–9, 132
fiction, views on, 18, 59–64, 83–4, 92–5
Fred Vincy, 17, 38, 149

gambling, 153–4
Gilfil, Mr, 29, 74
Grandcourt, 142, 152
Gwendolen, 74, 142, 152–5

Hackit, Mr, 95
Harold Transome, 122–3
Hayslope, 159, 164–5
Hetty Sorrel, 18, 38, 43–4, 74, 88, 96–102, 178
historical novels, 21, 108–14

Idea of a Future Life, The, 80
imagery, 98–101, 144
Irwine, Mr, 29, 38, 44, 97, 101–3

'Janet's Repentance', 30, 38, 95–6

Ken, Dr, 31
Klesmer, 74–5

Ladislaw, 55, 114, 123, 125, 143–6, 153
Lassman, Mr, 154
Letters (quoted), 23, 24–5, 39, 49, 53–5, 59–60, 65, 78–9, 96, 105, 171, 179
library, GE's, 162
Life of Jesus, The, 39–42, *and see* Strauss in General Index
'Lifted Veil, The', 34, 51
Loamshire, 164–5
'Looking Backward', 19
Lucy, 19, 107
Lydgate, 17, 44, 135, 139, 147–9, 171

Maggie Tulliver, 19, 31, 38, 73–4, 105–8, 117, 119, 141
manuscript, GE's, 162
Middlemarch, 11, 14, 16–18, 20, 22, 29–30, 33, 38–9, 70, 73, 80, 114, 119, 120, *123–7*, *130–51*, 152, 154, 156, 171, 182, 184
Middlemarch, 170
Milby, 30, 95, 170–1
Mill on the Floss, The, 13, 14, 17–21, 38, 67, 73–4, 88, *105–8*, 115, 116–9, 162–4, 176
Miss Brooke, 133–4
Mordecai, 75, 80, 152, 155–6
'Mr Gilfil's Love-Story', 29, 74, 95, 165

'Natural History of German Life, The', 28, 83–8, 90–1, 93, 101

'O may I join the choir invisible', 75–6, 80
'originals', 159

parables, 46–7
pastoral, 96
patterns and design in

novels, 101, 121–7, 131, 133–9, 152–4
periodical essays and reviews, 53, 60, 67, 69, 83–8, 179–80
Philip Wakem, 51, 74, 106
poetry, 19, 75–6
point of view, 102–3, 143
politics in novels, 114–5, 121–9, 151, 181
popularity of *Adam Bede*, 47, 101
Poyser, Martin, 44, 98, 170
Poyser, Mrs, 95, 98, 101
prose style, 86–7, 90–1, 103

'quarry' for *Middlemarch*, 133, 183

'Red Deeps, the', 170
Rome, 144–5
Romola, x, 22, 38, 65, 70, 91, *108–15*, 121, 132, 150, 182
Romola, 108–15, 132, 173

Rosamond Vincy, 20, 73–4, 134, 145, 148–9
Rufus Lyon, 20, 122

St Ogg's, 88, 162
Scenes of Clerical Life, 29–31, 68, 90, 92–6 *and see* separate stories
Seth Bede, 33, 159
Shepperton Church, 19, 88–91, 165
Silas Marner, 18, 33, 47, 66–7
'Silly Novels by Lady Novelists', 60, 69
Snowfield, 161
Spanish Gypsy, The, 75, 108, 121, 131, 155
Stephen, 74, 106–7
Stonyshire, 161
'Study of Provincial Life, A', 55, 121

Tessa, 108–9

Theophrastus Such, Impressions of, 19, 68, 76
time, 154–5
Tito, 38, 108–9, 114, 153
Transome, Mrs, 121–3, 146, 152
Treby Magna, 121, 165
Tryan, Mr, 30, 171
Tulliver, Mr, 17, 19, 21
Tulliver, Tom, 17, 19, 107, 117–9, 176, 184
Tyke, Mr, 30, 147–8

understatement, 95

Victorian novel, 95, 150–1
Vincy, Harriet, see Mrs Bulstrode, 146–7
Vincy, Mayor, 30, 135

Warwickshire scenes, 87, 121
'web', 139

Zionism, 155–6